URBAN HOMESTEADING FOR BEGINNERS

Starting Where You Are

Urban Homesteading for Beginners: Starting Where You Are

By Renee McCorry

TABLE OF CONTENTS

Chapter 14

Utilizing Sustainable Sources

Dedication

To all the urban dreamers who are turning their concrete jungles into thriving homesteads. May this book inspire you to create your own little piece of paradise, no matter how small your space.

Preface

As a child, I have vivid memories of plucking green beans and juicy vine-ripened tomatoes straight from my mother's garden. I would tiptoe along the rows, careful not to step on anything vital, and then dash inside excitedly, to proudly display my bountiful harvest.

Then there was the fig tree in the far-left corner of the yard, which never failed to flourish each year, growing into a magnificent fruit-laden sight.

My siblings and I would eat them right off the tree by the handfuls. I recall my mother saying she had planted it and never did anything to it. Yet every spring, it would bounce back larger and larger and dripping with fruit.

You may assume I was raised in a rural area, but that is not true. My early years were filled with games of hide and seek amidst trash cans and underneath cars on the bustling streets of Brooklyn, New York. We were pioneers of urban homesteading long before it became a popular trend. For our neighborhood, it was simply our way of life.

The rhythm of life in the city can be fast-paced and overwhelming. But among the towering buildings and bustling streets, a desire for nature and self-reliance often stirs within us.

This book is a testament to the power of urban homesteading, a step back into how things used to be done. Urban homesteading is a growing movement among city and suburb dwellers to reconnect with the earth and nurture their own food. I can tell you, it is possible even with limited space. As you read through these pages, you will find practical advice, inspiring stories, and basic techniques to guide you on your new journey to creating a thriving urban homestead.

Whether you are a seasoned gardener or a complete novice, we will explore different gardening techniques for small spaces, the rewards of raising backyard chickens, and the joy of preserving your very own harvest.

This book is not just about growing food; it is about embracing a more sustainable and fulfilling lifestyle. It is about finding peace and purpose in the heart of a chaotic city, connecting with nature, and taking control of your well-being while becoming self-reliant. Let's embark on this exciting adventure together!

Introduction

The idea of homesteading conjures images of sprawling farmlands and barns filled with livestock, requiring acres upon acres of land. But what if I told you that you could embrace the spirit of homesteading right in your own kitchen?

How about in your own backyard, even if you only have a small balcony or a tiny patch of soil?

Millennials are recognizing the benefits of small gardens. It allows them to form a deeper connection with their local ecosystem, reduce their carbon footprint, and maybe even save some money. Homesteading is a lifestyle and a mindset.

Urban homesteading is rapidly gaining momentum. It empowers city dwellers to create a more self-sufficient and sustainable lifestyle. It's about pulling that loaf of freshly baked bread from the oven or heating the milk on the stovetop to begin the process of making your own yogurt.

It's about embracing the beauty of growing your own food, realizing your ability to be less reliant on the grocery store, and eliminating pesticides and preservatives from your diet, even in the midst of concrete and steel.

My journey began in a little backyard in Brooklyn and followed me to the suburbs. When I grew up, and we moved into our little home. I decided then I would only plant trees and bushes that produced fruit. My flower beds contain medicinal flowers such as echinacea and lavender.

Basically, if we can't eat it, I don't grow it. We produce about 50% of our vegetables, preserve our food, recycle water, make our own cheese, and cook from scratch.

Our dream is to move to a rural area where we can grow more of our own fruits and vegetables and raise and hunt our own meat. But that didn't mean we had to wait to start homesteading. You don't have to wait, either.

There are so many levels of homesteading. Do not let your lack of acreage discourage you. This does not necessarily mean you must hold off until the timing and location are perfect.

Everyone needs to start somewhere. Growing herbs on the windowsill, cooking from scratch, or even composting your vegetable scraps are all steps to becoming more self-reliant.

This book is simply a guide for transforming your urban space into your very own thriving homestead, whether you are a seasoned gardener or a complete novice. We will explore techniques for maximizing space, like vertical gardening and raised gardens, and discover the joys of raising backyard chickens. You will learn the basics of how to preserve your harvest, ensuring that your homegrown, homemade goodness lasts all year round.

Are you motivated by a desire for fresh, healthy food? Do you yearn to connect with nature or have a passion for sustainable living? Are you tired of dozens of food recalls? If you can say yes to any of these questions, allow this book to guide you to creating a thriving homestead with little to no land.

I do not know everything about gardening, nor do I claim to know everything about homesteading. Every day, I learn something new about this lifestyle.

This book is a starter guide. There is so much more for you and me to learn and explore beyond these pages. But for now, we will start here. Get ready to unleash your inner homesteader and embark on an exciting journey of self-sufficiency and connection to the earth.

Chapter 1

The Appeal of Urban Homesteading

The pull of urban homesteading has blossomed into a growing popular movement, drawing individuals from all walks of life who crave a deeper connection with a more sustainable lifestyle. All a crossed the country, cities have been slowly transforming into a picture of green dreams, where rooftop gardens flourish, balconies overflow with herbs, and backyard chickens strut their feathery plumbs.

At the heart of this urban renaissance lies a desire for self-sufficiency, a yearning to break free from the industrial food system and embrace the simple pleasures of homegrown goodness. The allure of fresh produce, bursting with flavor but not tainted by pesticides, is a call to many urbanites seeking healthier eating habits and wanting a closer connection to the source of their food. Let's face it: Many of us have no idea what is used in growing our food.

The food industry uses a variety of additives and preservatives to keep food from decaying. For example, citric acid, a black mold grown organically in citrus fruits, is the most common preservative used in the world. Citric acid is not all bad. However, controlling the amount you consume should be your choice. Some other chemicals that can be found in our food today can include methylmercury, polychlorinated biphenyls (PCBs), polybrominated diphenyl ethers (PBDEs), bisphenol A (BPA), phthalates, perfluorochemicals (PFCs), perchlorate, and organophosphate pesticides.

Other countries refuse to allow such pollutants into their supermarkets. The United States is not so strict with the food supply. Even though PCBs were banned in the United States in the 1970s, they still cycle between air and soil and can accumulate in the leaves and parts of plants and food crops.

Doesn't sound very natural, does it? Or maybe you are thinking so what is it really going to hurt me?

It definitely can!

Let's start with your reproductive system. According to the National Institute for Health, exposure to these harmful chemicals at an early age profoundly impacts your reproductive system.

And not only are you affected, but also your descendants, as evidenced by recent research. The transmission of aberrant developmental traits across multiple generations, a phenomenon of significant consequence, is DNA modifications that regulate gene activity beyond the underlying sequence.

Polychlorinated biphenyls can cause acne and rashes. BPAs and PFCs can negatively affect cognitive and brain function, blood pressure, the immune system, and the body's ability to fight infection, cause liver damage, and are linked to multiple types of cancer. I know all this is pretty heavy stuff. It is a good motivation to do away with the national food industry. Homesteading offers peace of mind.

Beyond the culinary delights, urban homesteading offers a therapeutic escape from the relentless fast pace of city life. Studies have shown that gardening can help reduce depression, anxiety, and stress by nurturing plants and witnessing their growth.

From fragile seedlings that grow into satisfying harvests, there is a sense of accomplishment and deep satisfaction in growing gardens. The gentle breeze as you tend to the garden, the earthy scent of soil, and the soothingchirping of backyard birds create a sanctuary of tranquility away from the craziness of city life.

Urban homesteading is not merely about growing food; it is a lifestyle choice and an attempt to achieve self-sufficiency right where you are, using what you have. It's about taking control of your food choices and the environmental impact of everyday living. It's about avoiding genetically modified and bioengineered foods and embracing naturally grown vegetables and grass-fed meat.

This movement aligns perfectly with the growing global awareness of sustainability. It encourages individuals to reduce their carbon footprint by sourcing food locally and minimizing waste.

Overcoming Urban Challenges

Homesteading is an exciting and rewarding adventure but presents unique challenges in a city or small space environment. Limited yards or balconies and city and town ordinances can restrict what you can grow or raise.

My family and I experienced a county ordinance disrupting our journey not too long ago. I was gifted a dozen fertilized Silkie eggs and told I could eat or hatch them.

Seizing the chance to fulfill my long-standing wish for chickens, I secretly took them to the church daycare center and set up an incubator for the four-year-old class to hatch. Behold, twenty-two days later, ten adorable balls of fluff were hatched.

After confessing my secret hatching to my husband, we took them home and raised the chicks until they were big enough for our backyard.

Before they even made it outside, a county employee showed up after an anonymous complaint, and we were forced to rehome them or face legal action. The county deemed our quarter- acre property insufficient for raising chickens. One acre of land is required to raise poultry in my county. My chicken days were over… for now.

What did I learn? Right now, raising chickens is not in the cards. However, does this mean I can't enjoy freshly laid eggs? Not necessarily. I can still acquire the restricted items through other venues like farmer markets.

The good news is that with a little bit of creativity and resourcefulness, you can successfully overcome these challenges and create a thriving urban homestead.

Starting with Design

Designing your urban homestead can be as exciting as redesigning your home. As you embark on this new lifestyle, you will discover that there is so much more to it than simply growing vegetables.

Homesteading is about developing a deep connection with nature, even within the confines of a city. It is about embracing self-sufficiency and creating a peaceful place that nourishes both the soul and the body.

As you plan your urban homestead, you will navigate the unique challenges and opportunities that city living presents. This careful planning lays the foundation for a thriving and sustainable space, and this planning extends beyond the garden.

Space Constraints

The most obvious hurdle in urban homesteading is the lack of space. Tiny backyards, postage-stamp- sized balconies, and even just a windowsill are the canvas on which you will paint your urban homesteading dreams. But do not let limited square footage discourage you. The key to fitting more into less is to think vertically and utilize every inch of available space.

Vertical gardening techniques are your best friend in a space-constrained environment. Imagine transforming a plain wall into a lush living wall overflowing with herbs, vegetables, and flowers.

Container gardening is another option. Imagine hanging baskets cascading with vibrant flowers or rows of strawberry plants hanging from a trellis, stacked on the balcony, or hanging from the front porch. These techniques not only save valuable ground space but also create a stunning visual display.

Don't overlook spots, either. Think outside the box. What about planting thyme or catnip in between stone paths or broken pavement? Maintaining the area while the seedling is still sprouting may be challenging and will take some babying at first.

It is best to plant the young seedlings or seeds in crevices between March and May.

Even a sunny windowsill can be turned into a micro-garden, perfect for growing herbs or starting seeds. The fire escape is the perfect structure for pole beans or cucumbers. You can also use tiered planters or hanging baskets to create a mini garden on your balcony or patio.

Navigating City Regulations

City ordinances can be a bit of a maze, especially when it comes to homesteading practices. Many cities have restrictions on raising chickens, limiting how many beehives you own, and even composting. Water harvesting is encouraged in Texas, and tax incentives are offered. However, it is illegal to harvest water in Colorado.

Believe it or not, there really are laws in many cities and towns in the United States that forbid people from keeping edible gardens in their front yards.

Before you begin to plan your vegetable garden, verify that the property's deed restrictions do not prohibit or restrict altering the architectural aesthetic. This will ensure that your garden location does not lead to any penalties.

The key here is research and communication. Before embarking on your homesteading journey, take the time to understand your city's regulations.

Get familiar with your city's zoning laws. Determine if your property allows certain types of gardening and livestock on the property.
Check with your Homeowners' Association (HOA) If you live in a community with an HOA, they may have additional regulations governing your yard or balcony.

Consider community gardens. You will meet a

lot of like-minded people.

If space limitations are a concern, look for community gardens in your neighborhood. These shared spaces offer a fantastic way to connect with like-minded individuals and grow your own food.

Join local homesteading group**s.** Networking with other urban homesteaders can provide valuable guidance and direction on navigating local restrictions and regulations.

Noise Restrictions

City life can be noisy, and that includes your own backyard activities. Chickens can be vocal creatures, and even the buzz of a garden pump can be irritating to your neighbors. Respecting your neighbors' peace and quiet is essential for harmonious urban homesteading.

Choose quieter chicken breeds
Some breeds, like the Buff Orpington, are known for their quiet demeanor. Road Island Red chickens are docile and quiet and the Ameraucana are also moderately quiet.

Strategically place your coop:
Consider placing your coop in a secluded corner of your yard, away from your neighbors' homes.

Minimize the noise from equipment:
Use noisy garden tools and appliances during acceptable times whenever possible. Midnight drills interrupting your neighbor's sleep will not lead to an amicable relationship.

Communicate with your neighbors

Keep your neighbors informed about your homesteading activities and be open to their concerns. Happy neighbors will only be an asset to your plans.

Planning Your Urban Homestead

Designing your urban homesteading space is an exciting step. It isn't just about growing vegetables; it's about creating a sense of connection to nature, becoming more self-sufficient, and creating a space that nourishes your soul as much as your body. So, how do you go about designing this urban oasis? It begins with careful planning. First, consider your unique challenges and the opportunities in your environment.

Every aspect of your urban homesteading space should be intentionally designed to create a sanctuary that provides a sense of peace and fulfillment. It will be a place where you can escape the hustle and bustle of city life, connect with the landscape you created, and discover the joy and satisfaction of self-sufficiency. Start where you are!

Space Optimization: Making the Most of Your Urban Oasis

With buildings and houses built practically on top of each other, space is a precious resource in the city, so maximizing every inch is essential.

Vertical Gardening

Embrace vertical gardening. This technique allows you to grow plants up and down and frees up valuable ground space.

Raised Beds

Create raised beds to add height and structure to your garden. They also provide better drainage and nutrient-dense soil. Remember that raised beds can be placed on that unused driveway!

Box Gardens

Utilize box gardens to grow herbs, flowers, and even vegetables in smaller, more defined spaces. They are portable and can be arranged to suit your needs.

Container Gardening

Don't underestimate the power of container gardening. With the proper containers and plants, balconies and patios can be transformed into thriving gardens.

Compact Plant Choices

Select compact and dwarf varieties of plants and vegetables.

Designing for Sustainability: A Holistic Approach

Beyond the practical considerations of sunlight, water, and space, a truly sustainable urban homestead focuses on minimizing waste and helping develop a healthy ecosystem.

Composting
Start composting to create nutrient-rich soil amendments for your garden. Composting helps reduce waste and naturally enriches the soil.

Native Plants
Incorporate native plants to attract pollinators and beneficial insects. These plants require less care and thrive in the local climates.

Closed-Loop Systems
Explore closed-loop systems like aquaponics to grow fish and plants together. Imagine pulling out a fish for dinner after gathering herbs from the garden the system is feeding. These systems offer an efficient and sustainable approach to urban gardening.

Designing your urban garden is an exciting journey. It is a process that evolves your experience and learning. Don't be afraid to experiment, make mistakes, and adapt your design.

Embrace the Process:
Urban homesteading is a journey, not a destination. That saying may be overused, but in this case, it is true. Allow your space to evolve as you learn more about your environment, your plants, and your gardening style.

Sharing Your Passion:
Connect with other urban homesteaders in your community. Find your tribe! Sharing knowledge, experiences, and resources is a powerful way to learn and grow in your experience.

Documenting Your Journey:
Take photos, keep a journal, and share your progress with others. Your journey can inspire others to take steps toward self-sufficiency.

Embrace Creativity and Flexibility Overcoming urban homesteading challenges often requires creativity and flexibility.

Think outside the box, literally! Repurpose old dresser drawers and crates, or even turn tires into planters. Utilize vertical spaces with trellises and hanging baskets. Experiment with different growing methods, like hydroponics, to maximize space and water efficiency.

Finding Joy in the Journey

The journey of urban homesteading has its challenges, but the rewards are unlimited. Connecting with nature, enjoying fresh, home-grown produce, and contributing to a more sustainable lifestyle are just a few of the joys you will experience.

Remember, urban homesteading is about adapting to your environment, embracing a simpler lifestyle, and finding joy in the journey. Whether you're transforming a tiny balcony into a flourishing garden, raising a couple of backyard chickens, or simply starting a compost bin, every step you take contributes to a more sustainable and fulfilling life in the city.

The beauty of urban homesteading lies in its adaptability and creativity. You can transform a small balcony, a rooftop, or even a windowsill into a vibrant, self-sufficient space.

With a bit of planning, a lot of passion, and a commitment to sustainability, you can create an urban oasis that nourishes you, your community, and the planet.

Understanding Your Gardening Choices

Raised Beds: A Foundation for Success

Raised beds are a game-changer for urban homesteading. They offer a wealth of benefits, particularly in small urban spaces. First, they provide a raised planting area, giving your plants a head start by elevating them above potential soil- borne pests and diseases. Believe me, there is nothing worse than seeing your pumpkin plant begin to grow and watching the vibrant orange flower turn into a tiny pumpkin, only to have it destroyed by morning by a vicious vine borer.

Secondly, they allow you to control the soil composition, ensuring your plants thrive in a customized environment. You can choose a soil mix tailored to your specific crops, guaranteeing optimal drainage and nutrient content.

Additionally, raised beds make gardening more accessible, especially for those with mobility limitations. You can easily reach into the bed without straining, making gardening a comfortable and enjoyable experience.

Trellises: Climbing Towards Abundance

Trellises are essential tools for vertical gardening. They transform your limited space into a vertical garden of bounty. A lattice structure against a wall will provide support for climbing plants, such as beans, tomatoes, cucumbers, and even grapes. By directing plants upward, trellises maximize vertical space, allowing you to grow more in a smaller space.

Not only are trellises practical, but they can also add an element of visual appeal to your space. You can choose from many materials and styles, from simple wooden stakes to intricately crafted metal frames.

Trellises come in so many shapes and sizes, from small freestanding structures to large, wall-mounted systems. You will find the perfect option for your space.

Vertical Gardening Systems: Growing Upwards

Vertical gardening is a revolutionary approach to urban homesteading. It allows you to maximize your space and create a thriving garden even if you have limited space. Vertical gardening systems come in many forms, from simple DIY projects using recycled materials to more elaborate, commercially available structures.

Living walls, for instance, are popular for their eye-catching aesthetics and ability to transform vertical surfaces into living green walls.

These walls typically consist of modular panels that hold individual plant pots, allowing you to create a vibrant vertical garden. Another popular option is hanging baskets. They are perfect for balconies and patios. These baskets can be filled with a variety of herbs, flowers, and vegetables, adding greenery and freshness to your urban space.

Composting Bins: Turning Waste into Gold

Composting is a cornerstone of sustainable urban homesteading. It allows you to transform kitchen scraps and yard waste into nutrient-rich compost for your garden.

If you don't think you have the room to compost, think again. Composting bins are available in many sizes and materials, from small plastic rotating containers to large wooden structures.

They provide a controlled environment for the decomposition process. By adding kitchen scraps and brown matter to the bin, you will turn organic matter into valuable fertilizer. In addition, by composting your food scraps and yard waste, you reduce the amount of waste going to landfills, minimize your environmental footprint, and embrace a more sustainable lifestyle.

Pest Control: Protecting Your Plants

There are many types of pest control to choose from. Neem oil is a natural insecticide and fungicide that can help control pests and diseases in your garden. It is safe for plants and beneficial insects, making it a sustainable option for pest management.

Diatomaceous earth is a non-toxic insecticide that kills insects by dehydrating them. It is effective against a wide range of pests and can be sprinkled around plants or mixed into the soil.

Try to stick with using organic pesticides that are safe for humans and the environment. Always read the label carefully and follow the instructions for safe and effective use. Remember, the joy of urban homesteading lies in getting your hands dirty and connecting with nature in your own unique way.

Chapter 2
Tools of the Trade: Hand Tools

Choosing the Right Tools

The tools and equipment you choose will depend on your individual needs, preferences, and the size of your urban homestead. Take your time to research different options and consider your budget, space allowance, and the types of plants you want to grow. Don't be afraid to experiment with different tools to find what works best for you. As you become more experienced with your tools, you can gradually expand your collection, adding new tools and equipment as needed.

Remember, the joy of urban homesteading is the process of getting your hands dirty and taking a hands-on approach, all while using your own unique ideas.

With every homesteading journey, urban,

suburban, or otherwise, it is essential to equip yourself with the right tools to be able to nurture your city sanctuary easily. Here's a guide to the essential tools you'll need for urban gardening, including a mix of hand tools and mechanical aids.

Gardening Gloves

First, let's talk about hand tools that are necessary for any gardener. These are the tools you will use most often, so investing in good-quality, durable options is wise. Start with a sturdy pair of gardening gloves to protect your hands from dirt, thorns, and other irritants. I love to feel my hands deep in the soil. To work the earth barehanded and feel the roots of the plants as I put them in place. Or wrapping my hand around a sweet potato, knowing it is time to dig it up by just the feel of it.

Unfortunately, the red ants like to bite those hands that have inadvertently unsettled their nest. After a week of scratching and painful sores, I put the gloves on. At least until the next time I get the urge to play pioneer farmer.

Cotton gloves are lightweight and breathable. They are a good choice for gardening in warm weather.

Nitrile-coated gloves provide excellent grip and flexibility.

Pruning and rose gloves are designed to protect your hands from getting poked by thorns while pruning roses and other sharp plants and stems.

Heavy-duty gloves are cut and puncture-resistant. Your hand will be well-protected

Leather gloves are durable and offer excellent protection against thorns and other sharp objects.

Trowels

Next on my list are trowels. The hand trowel is a small, short-handled gardening tool often erroneously called a garden spade. They have a pointed cutting edge and tend to have a V-shaped or rounded blade to improve scooping and digging in tight spaces.

It should be close to your hand grip. I advise choosing a lightweight one. Even with larger hands, the biggest size trowel may not be the best choice, as less hand and wrist weakness means you can work at a steadier pace for a longer period of time and with a lower risk of injury.

A transplanting trowel has a slimmer blade than a hand trowel. The depth measurements marked on the tool allow you to accurately measure your soil. The slim head is designed to aid in transplanting small plants, perennials, and vegetables and is ideal for moving young plants with minimal root disturbance.

A **hand cultivator** or a three-pronged claw has, you guessed it, three elongated metal prongs in a claw-like shape. The rounded tines of the three- prong cultivator move through soil easily, aerating it while shallow-rooted weeds, and loosen the soil around uprooting weeds. It helps to break up soil, remove deep roots to make them easier to pull out.

Rake

Don't forget to pick up a sturdy rake to smooth out soil and collect garden debris. Choosing a rake is not always straightforward. Aluminum or fiberglass typically offer a great balance of durability and lightness, while wood and steel are viable but heavier alternatives.

A **dirt rake**, also called the garden or soil rake, is a vital tool for the vegetable or flower gardener. It has a long handle and a steel rake head with a solid steel tine set at a 90-degree angle to the rake head. The tine allows the user to loosen the soil and break up clumps of dirt. The tines come in straight or slightly curved under styles to help grab large dirt clods and other debris. After turning the soil, dirt rakes are used in the final step to prepare the garden before planting.

If you are going to be raking leaves, you will need a **leaf rake**, also known as a lawn rake. It is sold in different widths and has a long handle with tines that fan out in a triangle. The tines of a leaf rake are generally made of plastic, bamboo, or metal. Metal will last the longest but is not as effective as plastic rakes when you want to move large, wet piles of leaves. Leaf rake tines made of bamboo are fragile but are gentler on plants if you are raking garden beds.

The Shovel

There are so many options available. With over 36 types of shovels to choose from, which one is best suited for your individual garden? There is the sod shovel, the square shove, trenching shovels, mini shovels, root shovels, and the square point shovel.

A short-handled shovel is a perfect choice for urban gardeners with limited space. This type of shovel is typically smaller and lighter than its long-handled counterparts, making it easier to maneuver in tight spaces. The compact design allows you to store it in your tool shed or a container without taking up too much precious space.

When selecting your short-handled shovel, look for one with a durable metal head that can withstand various soil conditions. A pointed blade will be your best bet, as it can easily penetrate compacted dirt and clay-like textures, making planting and transplanting an easier task.

Be sure the handle has a comfortable grip with a non-slip material. If you have a little more storage space, you may also want to invest in a longer handled option for those times when you need to reach further, scoop mulch, or dig deeper without putting strain on your back. Having both options in your tool arsenal will ensure you're prepared for any gardening challenge that comes your way.

Pruning Sheers

A good pair of pruning shears will allow you to trim and shape your trees and bushes and encourage healthy growth.

Anvil pruners have one blade that pushes down onto a piece of metal or plastic to crush when they cut. They are best for cutting deadwood or making rough cuts on thicker, harder stems.

Bypass pruners have two separate curved blades that pass each other as you cut. One blade is very sharp, and the other is slightly duller. They are great for clipping green plant materials and harder plants. They are not as large as anvil pruners.

Ratchet pruners are a great substitute for anvil pruners for anyone with arthritis or a hand injury. Since there is one blade and it has a more "catch and hold" mechanism, it allows you to press down slightly multiple times to cut all the way through, putting less pressure on your wrist.

Loppers, in my opinion, are a must-have if you have trees or bushes with larger branches. The long handles require both hands to use. The curved scissor blade is a perfect tool to trim high branches.

It is not necessary to have all the pruning tools I have suggested. Select the ones that are most suitable for your specific situation. However, when shopping for pruning shears, be sure to choose a pair with a safety lock that keeps it shut when not in use. This will help protect the blade. Look for pruners with nonstick blades or a sap groove that can direct sap away from the blades to prevent them from sticking together.

And finally, for the best durability, look for

steel or titanium-coated blades. Your shears will need to be sharpened on occasion.

Watering Cans and Hoses

To keep your plants well hydrated and happy, invest in a good quality watering can with a long spout for targeted watering. Select the watering can perfect for your needs by considering its intended use. Consider your gardening plans. Will you primarily be watering vertically? In that case, opt for a lightweight and smaller watering can to help avoid straining when lifting it high to water hanging or elevated plants. Is the can comfortable to carry, and is it the correct size to use around your home and garden?

For outdoor watering, consider durable and lightweight, and for indoor use, look for a smaller capacity with a long spout for accurate and consistent water flow, avoiding any splashing.

Like shovels, the variety of hose options available can be overwhelming. These options include hoses that are kink-resistant and those with added microbial protection.

Rubber hoses are known for their durability and flexibility. Many homeowners love the ease of maneuvering rubber hoses around their gardens and properties. Rubber hoses are heavier than vinyl hoses but are flexible.

Vinyl and vinyl-reinforced hoses are inexpensive, lightweight, and easy to handle. Reinforced hoses stand up to temperature changes better than other types of hoses and are less likely to kink or burst.

Plastic hoses are not as well-known as their vinyl or rubber counterparts, but they offer a variety of benefits. They are inexpensive, flexible, and safe for drinking water. The reinforced types are heavy-duty and kink-resistant. Plastic hoses are commonly used for RVs and boats.

A **soaker hose** is porous and can be buried under a layer of mulch. The hose drips water directly into your garden or flower bed, keeping the plant leaves dry and free from developing leaf diseases with little waste. A soaker hose provides deep watering as the water soaks directly into the ground.

Sprinkler hoses are designed to be used on the ground surface and are punctured with holes on one side to spray water upwards gently. Like the soaker hose, they are very convenient, and with a turn of the water spigot, your garden irrigation is underway.

Now, if you have the storage space, let's move on to some larger tools that will help make your urban gardening more efficient.

Wheelbarrow

A good old-fashioned wheelbarrow is perfect for hauling soil, compost, and rocks around your space. First, determine your needs. There are three main types of wheelbarrows: the utility, garden, and dump.

The **garden barrow** is small but still has enough room to handle landscaping tasks such as planting flowers or moving mulch. It's also easier to lift due to its smaller size and lighter weight.

Dump barrows are larger than other types so that they can hold more material, and they have wider tires, which make it easier to push over uneven ground.

Remember, part of the joy of your homestead journey is discovering what works best for you and your space. Do not be afraid to start small and adapt as you go!

Chapter 3
Vertical Gardening: Maximizing Small Spaces

Vertical gardening is more than just a trend; it is a revolutionary approach to growing food and greenery in limited spaces. It's an art that transforms plain fences, brick walls, and even plain rooftops into vibrant horticulture masterpieces. Can you imagine your tiny balcony bursting with tomatoes, peppers, and herbs or the unused rooftop blooming with flowers and vegetables? Vertical gardening unlocks the potential of vertical surfaces. By using this technique, you can maximize your space and create a productive and stunning garden.

At its core, vertical gardening is all about using vertical space to support plant growth. This technique offers numerous benefits for urban dwellers, making it an ideal solution for those with limited square footage.

Visual Appeal

Vertical gardening is not only about being practical; it is also about aesthetics. Just imagine a wall covered in cucumber vines, fragrant herbs, and colorful flowers that will later be turned into medicine for you and your family. These green walls bring nature to even the most urban environments.

They can transform concrete jungles into lush gardens, bringing life and beauty into a dull and boring space.

Think of the impact a living wall can have on your kitchen. What about an herb garden in your bathroom or a bright flower wall on your balcony? Vertical gardens can add charm and character to any urban space.

Minimizing Soil Volume

Another remarkable advantage of vertical gardening is its ability to minimize soil volume. Traditional gardening often requires large amounts of soil, which can be heavy and difficult to manage, especially in urban settings. Vertical gardening systems use smaller amounts of soil. The amount of soil needed is decreased, and the entire process is much more manageable. This benefits apartment dwellers, who might struggle with carrying heavy bags of soil up flights of stairs.

Vertical gardening is not just a whimsical idea; sound scientific principles support it. When light, air soils are used in vertical structures like trellises, the airflow and ventilation are ideal. This open-air circulation helps prevent diseases and pests from spreading and ensures healthy and productive plant growth.

Vertical gardens also allow better sunlight exposure since the plants are not shaded by their balcony walls.

Beyond Space-Saving: A Sustainable Approach

Vertical gardening is not only about squeezing more plants into smaller spaces but also about adopting a more sustainable approach to gardening.

Reducing the amount of soil used can significantly decrease water usage since less soil needs to be hydrated. Conserving water is a major advantage, especially in cities with water restrictions.

Additionally, vertical gardening promotes natural pest control by attracting beneficial insects and reducing the need for chemical pesticides. By reducing your dependence on harmful chemical fertilizers, you are contributing to a healthier environment and producing more nutritious, free-of-toxins food for your family.

Plants for Vertical Gardens

Vertical gardening opens a world of possibilities when it comes to plant selection. You can cultivate a wide range of plants, from leafy greens and tomatoes to vibrant flowers and herbs. The key is to choose plants that flourish in vertical environments, considering their growth habits, light requirements, and overall size. Above all, choose plants that will benefit your household.

To achieve a thriving vertical garden, it is essential to select the system right for you and your home and design it to succeed. Factors like sunlight exposure, drainage, and the specific needs of your chosen plants should also be considered.

Vertical Gardening Systems: A Diverse Array of Options

Vertical gardening systems come in so many different sizes, shapes, colors, and materials, each with its own advantages and limitations. Let's take a closer look at some popular choices:

Living Walls

Living walls are systems that use panels covered in growing media like soil, peat moss, or rockwool, where plants are grown in pockets or containers. These walls can be self-supporting or built into other vertical structures. They are beautiful and perfect for creating a diverse garden. Keep in mind that they can be difficult to install and maintain.

Trellises

Trellises are classic vertical gardening structures. They provide support for climbing plants like grapes, beans, tomatoes, and flowering vines. They come in a variety of styles and materials, like vinyl and wood. Trellises offer a simple and efficient way to maximize vertical space. They are also pretty DIY-friendly, which allows you to create a system custom to your needs.

Hanging Baskets

Hanging baskets offer a charming option for a vertical garden. They can be hung from balconies, patios, and even indoors! They add a touch of color to any space. Hanging baskets are ideal for draping plants like strawberries, herbs, and flowering vines. The key is to ensure proper drainage and choose plants that can thrive in a hanging environment.

Tiered Planters

As the name suggests, Tier planters feature multiple levels of plants stacked vertically. They provide a compact and efficient way to grow different types of plants in a small space. Tiered planters also come in many styles. They can be made from materials such as wood, plastic, or metal and offer a modern, stylish approach to vertical gardening.

The Vertical Gardening Journey: From Planning to Planting

Now that you understand the basic concept of vertical gardening, let's take a look at building and maintaining your personal vertical homestead. The process can be broken down into the following steps:

1. Planning and Design

Begin by assessing your space. How? Start by measuring how much space you have to work with. Consider sunlight exposure, where the closest water source is, and what vertical gardening system best suits your style and needs. Create a plan that incorporates the plants you chose and the vertical structures you will be using.

2. Choosing the Right Plants

Select plants that will be useful to you and your family, grow well in vertical environments, and complement your design. Consider their growth habits, need for light, and space requirements.

3. Building Your Vertical System

There are many excellent pre-made vertical garden systems on the market. You can also build your own, especially if you are working with unusually shaped areas. Use materials such as wood, metal, or recycled items. Check that your system provides the necessary support needed for your chosen plants and has proper drainage.

4. Planting and Care

Here comes the fun part. Once your system is ready, sow your seeds and put them in your plants. Follow the spacing and correct depth instructions given on seed packages and plant tags. You will need to water the plants and seeds regularly.

Fertilize plants when needed and look out for any signs of pests or disease.

5. Maintenance and Harvesting

Maintain your vertical garden by providing consistent watering, fertilization, and pruning as needed. Harvest your produce regularly; the more you harvest, the more it will produce.

Vertical gardening allows you to grow your own food and creates a beautiful and sustainable space.

Whether you are transforming a small balcony into the mini garden of your dreams or adding a splash of greenery to your rooftop, vertical gardening can transform your urban space into a stress-free, relaxing garden.

Types of Vertical Gardening Systems

Vertical gardening is a game-changer for urban homesteaders. It offers the solution to small spaces. It is like harnessing the power of gravity to transform your small patch of land or balcony into a bountiful mini farm. There's a vertical gardening system for every space and every style.

If you don't find what you like, take the step and learn to build it. Homesteading of any kind is all about learning and progressing.

Living Walls: Nature's Vertical Tapestry

Can you imagine a lush, living wall of plants replacing traditional wall art? A drab wall transformed into a bright green masterpiece? Living walls are not just beautiful; they are ecological powerhouses and offer numerous benefits to urban gardeners.

Space Maximization -They are the ultimate space savers, allowing you to grow more plants using less space.

Aesthetic Appeal – They bring beauty and add a touch of nature and color to your urban landscape.

Environmental Benefits—They help improve air quality, reduce noise pollution by blocking sound, and create an inviting environment.
With so many options for creating living walls, the choices are endless!

You can choose:

Modular Systems - Consists of prefabricated modules that fit together to create a wall. Often, they include built-in irrigation systems and drainage.

DIY Walls - For the adventurous homesteader, building a DIY living wall can be a rewarding project. You can use various materials, such as recycled pallets, wire mesh, or even repurposed wood.

Choose the right plants for your needs. The key to a successful living wall is selecting plants that thrive in vertical environments, such as vines and natural climbers. Trailing plants like strawberries add a cascading effect to the wall. You can never go wrong placing herbs such as thyme, basil, or oregano in the garden.

Rosemary is another wonderful choice, but it can grow as large as a bush and take up a lot of root space. Maintaining a living wall requires regular watering, fertilizing, and occasional pruning to keep it looking and growing its best.

Trellises: The Beauty of Vertical Growth

Trellises are simple but elegant structures that provide vertical support for climbing plants. They are a versatile option for urban gardens and offer various benefits.

Easy to Construct - Trellises like living walls can be easily built from a variety of materials, such as wood, metal, or even bamboo.

Versatile Support -They can be used to support a wide range of plants, from tomatoes and green beans to cucumbers and grapes.

Aesthetic Appeal -Trellises add a touch of rustic charm and elegance to any garden space. There are multiple types of trellises, each offering a unique design and functionality.

A-Frame Trellises:
These are classic trellises built to provide a strong, stable structure for tall climbing plants.

Oblique Trellises:
These types of trellises are angled trellises offering a more modern and stylish look.

Arched Trellises:

Arched trellises are perfect for creating a romantic walkway or entrance and provide a beautiful support structure for climbing roses or vines.

Choosing the Right Plants

Selecting plants with vining habits is crucial for trellises. Try planting indeterminate tomato varieties. They climb readily and produce a large number of flavorful fruits. Pole beans, like Kentucky Wonder or Blue Lake, are easy to find, produce a high yield, and are ideal for trellises.

Vining cucumbers produce a delicate yellow flower that explodes into juicy cucumbers. Certain types of cucumbers, like Persian or English cucumbers, love to climb and will reward you with baskets full of vegetables.

Trellises require minimal maintenance and typically require occasional pruning to control growth and ensure proper airflow.

Hanging Baskets: Waterfall of Colour

Hanging baskets are charming and add a touch of whimsical to any space. They are like colorful floating gardens, dangling from balconies and porches. They can even be hung indoors, creating a beautiful and inviting atmosphere. What are the benefits of hanging baskets?

They are perfect for maximizing vertical space, adding a touch of greenery and color without taking up valuable ground area. They are versatile and can accommodate a wide range of plants, from bushy lettuce to lush herbs and other small vegetables. Mostly, hanging baskets are easy to maintain and access for watering, fertilizing, and pruning.

Types of Hanging Baskets

Wire Baskets - These durable baskets are available in various sizes and offer excellent drainage.

Plastic Baskets - Lightweight and affordable plastic baskets are popular for hanging gardens.

Coir Baskets - Made from natural coconut fibers, these baskets provide good drainage and are a sustainable option.

Tiered Planters: A Stairway to Green Abundance

Tiered planters are like miniature vertical gardens. By stacking plants in tiers, they create a staircase of green and maximize space. These planters offer a stylish scene for your plants, adding a touch of elegance to any urban garden.

The benefit of using tiered planters in your landscape is for space efficiency. They make the most of limited space, allowing you to grow multiple plant types in a small footprint. They also create a beautiful visual display, adding interest to any garden.

Finally, tired planters are easy to maintain and allow easy access for fertilizing and watering plants.

Types of Tiered Planters

Wooden Tiered Planters—These planters offer a rustic, natural look and add warmth to any outdoor space.

Metal-Tiered Planters—These durable planters have a modern look and are a popular choice for contemporary gardens.

Plastic Tiered Planters—These planters are made

of lightweight plastic and are practical and affordable. They are a great option for urban gardeners just getting started.

Choosing the Right Plants

Herbs – Herbs grown in planters can be unlimited and include basil, oregano, thyme, and parsley. They are wildly viral, growing in tiered planters.

Small Vegetables—Lettuce, spinach, and radishes are perfect for this space. They are short-rooted, fast-growing, and do not require a lot of space.

Flowers - Colorful flowers like petunias, geraniums, and zinnias add a vibrant touch to tiered planters. Purple cone flowers, also known as echinacea, are an excellent choice for a pop of color and useful medicinal properties.

Stacked Planters: A Vertical Symphony of Growth

Vertical gardens can also be achieved using stacked planters, which provide a convenient and effective solution to small-space gardening.

These compact vertical farms optimize limited space in urban environments.
Stacked planters are beneficial and are a popular choice for small spaces. Here's why:

Space Maximization

Stacked planters make the most of vertical space by allowing you to grow more plants in a smaller area.

Easy to Assemble

These planters require minimal tools and are usually easy to assemble. Some styles have a click- together system.

Versatility

They can be used to grow a wide variety of plants, from herbs and flowers to vegetables and succulents.

For longer-lasting options, consider metal stacked planters. They are heavy-duty and offer a sleek and contemporary look. If you prefer the country look, wooden stacked planters can bring warmth and rustic charm to your patio

Choosing the Right Plants.

Herbs -Stacked planters are perfect for growing. Basil, oregano, thyme, mint, and parsley grow well in these planters.

Small Vegetables - Lettuce, spinach, arugula, kale, radishes, and even Asian greens thrive in these containers. It is best to choose varieties that have similar growing conditions so they all thrive together.

Small Berries—Strawberries and pineberries are excellent additions that will thrive and re-grow in tiered planters year after year. Drop cherries are charming berries resembling a Chinese lantern wrapped in delicate paper like a tomatillo. They are sweet to taste and great in salads and jam.

Wall-Mounted Planters: A Tapestry of Leaves

Wall-mounted planters transform your walls into a verdant tapestry. They are a clever way to create a living wall without needing a complicated system. There are many wall-mounted planters available. You can choose whimsical gnome mask planters or classic white resin depending on your taste and design.

Plastic Wall-Mounted Planters - Affordable and lightweight plastic planters are a popular choice for wall gardens.

Metal Wall-Mounted Planters - Durable and modern, metal planters offer a stylish and contemporary look.

Wooden Wall-Mounted Planters - Rustic and charming wooden planters add a touch of warmth to any space. By using the same variety of fruits and vegetables mentioned for the stacked planter, you can ensure the success of your chosen produce.

Caring for your tiered planters, stacked gardens, and wall-mounted planters requires monthly fertilizing for healthy growth.

Water regularly to ensure all plants receive enough moisture and nutrients.

Vertical Gardening: Embracing the Vertical Dimension

Vertical gardening is more than just a space-saving technique. It's a revolution in urban homesteading, allowing you to create a beautiful and productive mini-food farm in a limited space.

By embracing the concept of height, a whole new realm of opportunities opens up, transforming your bland concrete surroundings into a thriving green haven.

Will you choose a living wall, trellises, hanging baskets, tiered planters, or wall-mounted planters? Your vertical gardening choices will open a new world of creativity and food abundance. The joys of nature will be right on your doorstep.

Choosing Plants for Vertical Gardens

Choosing the right plants for your vertical garden is like casting a play. You need the perfect actors to fill the roles. What part will your flowers play in your urban homestead? Will the potted fruit trees or a rainbow of red, yellow, and purple tomatoes take center stage?

However, it's not only about beauty; it's about each plant's usefulness to your lifestyle and how they'll grow more abundantly and help feed your family.

Think of your vertical garden as a miniature ecosystem. Your garden will be made up of organic matter like wood, soil, mulch, stones, and water. Each growing medium plays an intricate role in the ecosystem's delicate balance.

Just as some creatures find solace in the ocean's depths, others thrive in the sun-drenched desert. Plants are no different. They each have specific and different needs for light, water, and space, and they will let you know if their needs are not being met.

To help your garden thrive, evaluate your space. Think about the energy it needs to grow and produce food. If your vertical garden is in direct sunlight for most of the day, you're in luck! A world of heat-loving vegetation such as tomatoes, peppers, and basil becomes a possibility for your plant selection.

However, if your vertical garden sits in a shadier spot, you still have options. Plenty of edible plants can thrive in low light or partial shade. Think salad! Leafy greens like lettuce, spinach, and kale prefer cooler temperatures and can handle lower light conditions. You can also cultivate herbs like cilantro, parsley, and mint, which are known for their resilience and ability to adapt to varying levels of sunlight.

Next, consider the growth habits of the plants you have chosen. Tomatoes climb upwards and should be trained to grow vertically on trellises or stakes. Others, like strawberries, prefer to spread out and might be better suited for hanging baskets or tiered planters. Before you commit to a plant, research its growth habits to be sure it's a good fit for your vertical gardening system.

Another key factor is space constraints. Vertical gardening maximizes space, but that doesn't mean you should cram every plant imaginable onto your walls.

Each plant has its own growth and space needs. Lettuces and herbs can be grown closely together, while tomatoes need more breathing room. Keep these space requirements in mind when planning your garden layout.

Tips for Choosing the Right Plants

Consider your climate

Different plants thrive in different climates. Research the hardiness zones for your area and select plants suited to your local conditions.

Think about your preferences

Do you prefer leafy greens, fruits, or herbs? Choose plants that you enjoy eating and that will enhance your culinary experience. If you aren't going to eat them, don't waste your time or space growing them.

Research your plants

Before you spend your hard-earned money on plants, research their specific needs. You will want to know their light requirements, growth habits, and space requirements.

Ask for advice

If you are unsure of something, ask! Don't hesitate to seek advice from experienced gardeners or local nurseries. They can provide valuable information and recommendations based on your needs and growing zone.

Experiment

Vertical gardening is a wonderful way to experiment with different plants and find your favorites. Every year, I try to grow something new. Do not be afraid to try growing that unusual carrot or strange-colored tomato. If it doesn't suit you, don't grow it again. However, you may find a hidden treasure perfect for your family.

Remember that choosing the right plants for your vertical garden is a vital step in creating a full and thriving garden. So, get creative, explore your options, and let your vertical garden bloom vibrant with life!

Chapter 4
Box Gardens and Raised Beds

Perhaps a Vertical Garden isn't your cup of tea. When asphalt and concrete dominate, box gardens and raised beds are perfect choices.

Box gardens are like miniature ecosystems, often taking the form of decorative planters. They are perfect for small spaces and can be placed on patios, balconies, or even rooftops. Imagine creating a collection of box gardens, each with its own unique theme and style. Some may be growing herbs and vegetables, while others could be filled with colorful flowers for herbal medicine.

I was excited when I began my journey into box gardening and raised beds. I knew that with some creativity and effort, I could transform my concrete-covered, poorly soiled space into a vibrant and productive garden. The options for box garden materials are diverse, each offering its own advantages and disadvantages.

Cedar or redwood is traditionally used for its natural beauty and durability. Concrete is often used due to its longevity and resistance to rot. However, it does have the potential for cracking.

If you are looking for an eco-friendly option, you could opt for recycled plastic, which offers a sustainable alternative in a variety of colors and sizes. However, you should consider the concerns about the potential leaching of harmful substances from recycled materials.

There are so many choices and a wealth of online knowledge on urban homestead gardening. I can only share the basics with you. Select your desired plants and hone your research to your preferences. Gradually add to your garden. Slowly add another vegetable or an unusual herb, incorporating a new flavor to your palate.

Raised beds and box gardens are perfect alternatives to the Vertical Garden when the soil is unsuitable for planting or when concrete covers the majority of your property.

A box garden, simply put, is a mini garden contained within a box or a container. It can be as small as a windowsill herb garden or as large as a waist-high planter. The beauty of a box garden is in its versatility. They can be placed anywhere, from balconies and rooftops to patios and driveways.

Box gardens can be designed to be at the perfect and comfortable height for someone with mobility issues, eliminating the need for bending or kneeling.

Box gardens seemed like the perfect solution to my nutrient-dense soil. I could have little plots of herbs, health-beneficial flowers, and vegetables popping up all over the place. And the best part? I could make them out of just about anything I have on hand. The hoarder, I mean the frugal collector in me, was yelling, "Finally, I can use those pallets I hide from my husband."

Raised beds, on the other hand, are larger structures that sit above the ground. They can be made from a variety of materials, such as wood, stone, or brick, and are filled with a rich mixture

of soil and compost. Since this type of soil is loose and well-drained, it is the perfect environment, giving plant roots ample room to grow. A raised bed design also makes it easier on the gardener's back and knees, eliminating the need to bend or stoop.

Both raised beds and box gardens offer numerous benefits, especially in an urban setting. They provide a controlled environment, allowing gardeners to create the perfect growing conditions for their plants. The soil mixture can be customized to suit the needs of specific plants, ensuring they thrive.

How about going with a quirkier box garden and expressing your unique style? Beyond the usual wood or plastic, you can get creative with materials like old bathtubs, repurposed barrels, vintage suitcases, and even an old dresser. Some people embrace the rustic charm of weathered metal troughs or galvanized buckets, while others might use something more whimsical, like colorful ceramic pots or painted terracotta planters.

Upcycling materials like old tires, pallets, or even broken concrete blocks can add a touch of industrial chic.

Once I decided on my own creative (and a bit chaotic) backyard plan, it was time to start dumpster diving! Old milk crates, wooden boxes, you name it. I scoured the streets for discarded treasures, and soon enough, I had a collection of potential garden boxes.

Now, this is where things got interesting. I like to think of myself as a bit of a green fairy in the garden. So, I started experimenting with soil blends, dried banana peels, egg shells, and composted coffee grinds. I was determined to create the perfect growing medium for my little box gardens. Let's just say it involved a lot of trial and error. I once read talking to plants helps them to grow. So, each day, I whispered encouragement to my little seedlings to grow big and tall.

What I'm try to say is to think outside the box (pun intended). Consider building your box garden from old windows or even a discarded boat hull. The possibilities are endless, and the only limit is your imagination!

Raised Beds

Raised beds are basically miniature gardens built above the ground. They create a contained and controlled environment for plants to grow and thrive. They are perfect for areas with poor soil or areas that lack soil. They can be filled with rich, nutrient-dense soil to encourage their growth. Building these above the ground also provides good drainage and allows for earlier planting and a longer growing season. Additionally, these gardens are a great way to make efficient use of space, as they can be designed to fit any area, no matter how small or unusual.

You may be wondering if you will ever use raised beds. Well, my friend, they are my go-to and main garden design. If you thought the story ended with me scavenging the streets like a gardening ninja, you are in for a treat. Because the real adventure began when I started constructing my raised beds.

So, do you want to hear about the great garden build of 2019?

Well, pull up a chair and let me tell you a tale of soil, sweat, and (very little) triumph. "Raised beds and box gardens," they said. "It'll be a breeze," they said. Well, let me tell you, when your backyard is more concrete jungle than lush paradise, you have got to learn how to get creative. And that is exactly what I did.

My heart was set on raised garden beds. I was tired of eating flavorless vegetables covered in chemicals and decided to take a step in reclaiming control over my food choices. I was going to transform my small yard into the green space of my dreams. I was determined to use the pallets I had secretly been collecting and hiding from my husband.

I mean, who wants to spend a fortune on store- bought materials when you can go on a treasure hunt in your own neighborhood?

Now, I have always considered myself a bit of a DIY enthusiast. I grabbed my husband's drill and set out eagerly to get this project started. Until he spotted me. You see, my dear spouse knows the truth: I'm a klutz. He promptly stopped me and took the drill from my accident-prone hands, and insisted he would build my DIY idea. He was the brawn, and I was the brains. I explained to him all the things raised beds could be made from: chicken wire and landscape fabric, cinderblocks, or galvanized metal.

I grew very excited, sharing with him the potential of pallets and how they could be used in the project, "they are cheap, actually free in some cases, and the perfect choice." Then he asked, "Where are they?" I had inadvertently revealed I had a secret stash.

All didn't go as well as I imagined. Using the pallets to build the raised beds was like assembling a giant puzzle after the dog ate a few pieces. After a few choice words from my husband, he went to the hardware store, brought home some 2-foot- wide by 8-foot-wide by 10-foot-long pieces of lumber, and got to building my first raised bed.

Meanwhile, I sanded, scrapped, de-nailed, and sealed those bad boys until those pallet pieces were transformed into rustic-chic trestles. Which later became a trellis and tiered planters that attached to the end of the garden bed.

My garden's first bed holds a special place in my heart. I can still recall the moment I plucked a ripe tomato, a crisp cucumber from the vine, and fresh romaine lettuce from the planter on my patio. I was a garden fairy who grew and crafted my very first salad entirely from my own garden!

That, my friends, is a feeling of satisfaction that no amount of store-bought, chemical-covered, waxed produce can ever replicate. So, the next time someone tells you gardening is a breeze, as you wipe the sweat from your brow, remember that it's a labor of love, but the rewards are oh-so-worth-it!

Today, that one garden bed has grown to nine raised beds and an array of vertical trestles and arches. It took a few years of learning and adding to my garden to get it exactly how I envisioned. It is not always easy, but there is pride in knowing, and I grew that and fed my family. Ultimately, the "best" material depends on personal preferences, budget, and the garden's specific needs.

Size Matters

It's time to move on to serious matters. Let's talk about size. A raised bed should be 3 to 4 feet wide and should accommodate any length of your garden. The most important rule to remember when selecting a size is to be sure you can access the bed from all sides to reach the center without stepping into it and crushing all your hard work.

As for the length, 8 feet is ideal, allowing you to grow small varieties of herbs and vegetables. The length can be shorter, doubled, or even tripled, but longer than 24 feet is not very practical. It is better to have several 8-foot beds that allow you to walk between them, giving you the access you need. With separate boxes, it is also easier to crop rotate each season, keeping heavy feeders away from each other and not reusing the same soil for other nightshades(peppers, tomatoes, eggplant). It also allows the grouping of plants with similar watering needs together.

Although it may seem space-efficient to place your beds closely together, leaving at least a foot of space between them is recommended to ensure comfortable walking access.

Prepare your box gardens and raised beds by layering organic materials such as branches, newsprint, leaves, and logs. This technique reduces the amount of soil needed and allows for the gradual decomposition of the materials, resulting in nutrient-rich compost for your plants.

Soil

Soil depth depends on the plants you select. Shallow-rooted crops like lettuce, spinach, and kale require a minimum soil depth of 6 inches, while deep-rooted crops like peppers, tomatoes, and carrots need at least 36 inches of soil.

If the soil in the raised bed is high-quality, the roots will grow deeper into the soil, establishing a stronger root system and stronger stems. This will allow optimal crop growth and development.

The trinity of garden bed soil uses a combination of compost, topsoil, and organic matter. Sand or grit can also be used. A good rule of thumb is to mix two parts of topsoil with one part of compost if this is the first time filling the beds.

However, if your beds already have soil, add 4 to 6 inches of compost after each seasonal use. You will want to add organic matter like recycled leaves, wood ash from the fire pit, and dehydrated chicken or cow manure to feed the soil. Continue to feed your plants with fertilizer as directed on the packaging.

Just as you and I need food to survive and thrive, your plants do as well. There is so much information and knowledge on urban gardening and homesteads that it would be impossible for me to share it all with you. I can offer advice and encourage you to choose the right plants for you.

Then, instruct you to direct your research around your selections. Learn everything you can about them. Slowly add other vegetables and other herbs to your garden.

Once you have your basic vegetables growing, incorporate an unusual herb, medicinal flower, or vegetable into your garden, customizing your "mini" farm to your personal needs.

Chapter 5
Community Gardens: Engaging with Community

There are more options than just vertical gardens. Sometimes, they are not viable. Urban homesteading takes a little bit of ingenuity and a whole lot of imagination.

The urban homesteading movement creates a close-knit and lively community where individuals come together in shared spaces like community gardens. A plot of soil is assigned. Sometimes, this requires a rental fee and, other times, a share of the crop. However, if this is the case, it is well worth it. If you can find a community garden in your area, I urge you to get involved.

These green spaces are hubs for social interaction, allowing friendships to blossom and a sense of self-reliance to thrive. They provide like-minded people the opportunity to work together towards a common goal. Community gardens not only bring people together but also build relationships, encourage teamwork, and promote sustainability.

Other urban homesteaders can share their knowledge with others. It becomes a place where seeds and surplus harvests are shared. This little community can provide you with a vast network of knowledge and support. It is beautiful when you see others coming together to support each other and work towards a shared goal to embrace sustainability. These green spaces allow you to see the collective effort between these gardeners and the strong bond they have built with each other.

The urban homesteaders' shared passion and dedication to achieve a sustainable lifestyle is shown in these community gardens. It's a sight that inspires others to pick up a shovel and start digging. It brings a sense of hope for a cleaner future.

As I researched the urban homesteading movement, I discovered that community gardens were its lifeblood. These hills of soil are scattered across the city, and they bring people together from all walks of life.

There is a particular garden between several warehouses that had been transformed into loft apartments.

I found a lively group of individuals tending to their assigned garden plots. All around me, there was conversation and laughter as they shared tips on compost mixtures and swapped stories about their first harvests. What struck me most was the sense of camaraderie and their openness to share.

These city gardeners became something more as they offered excess produce to their neighbors, creating a spontaneous farmers' market right there in the city! A young couple barter their surplus tomatoes for a basket of cucumbers from an elderly woman, who proudly displayed her grandson's artwork alongside her vining plants.

These community gardens are a place of learning and mentorship. Seasoned urban homesteaders guided newbies through the intricacies of organic pest control and soil preparation.

I listened in on a passionate discussion about the benefits of companion planting. Using basil and marigolds was encouraged as natural deterrents against unwanted insects. It was a beautiful display of intergenerational knowledge, with each gardener adding their unique twist to the collective wisdom.

Locating a Community Garden

You may ask, where are these gardens located? I have never come across one. Remember the slogan "let your fingers do the walking?"

Google "community gardens near me"- it is simple to do and a great start.

Check with your local parks and recreation department-They may have a wait list.

Visit the national website of https://www.CommunityGarden.org. - This site provides a comprehensive list of community gardens across the county.

The homesteading movement is about more than just growing vegetables or preserving food; it's about reclaiming a sense of self-sufficiency and food security, fostering community, reducing carbon imprints, and embracing a greener, eco-friendly way of life.

As urban and suburban spaces continue to evolve, the urban homesteading movement continues to grow, offering a path toward a healthier, happier, and more environmentally conscious life.

Chapter 6
Hydroponic Gardening: Urban Homesteaders Secret Garden

Some individuals do not have indoor or outdoor areas at their disposal. Perhaps there is no room for multiple containers, or there is not enough adequate sunlight. There are still possibilities to grow herbs, lettuce, and even miniature tomatoes.

For those with limited space and sunlight, hydroponic gardening is a game-changer. It is a method of growing plants without soil, using nutrient solutions in a water solvent.

What does this mean? Regardless of their living situation, anyone can become an urban farmer. With hydroponics, you can have a lush garden in a space as small as a tabletop.

The beauty of hydroponic gardening is its versatility. A small drip system can be set up on a tray table in the corner. The plants grow quickly and healthily, reaching towards the plant light as though it is natural sunlight.

Imagine plucking fresh basil leaves for your pasta or snipping chives to garnish your morning eggs. Even in the heart of the city, with the hustle and bustle of cars and buses rushing down busy streets, you can find peace in a hydroponic garden.

You nurture your plants and watch them grow and flourish. There is satisfaction in knowing that you are making an effort to improve your lifestyle.

Each small harvest will bring a sense of pride and a delicious reward for your efforts. Let's take a look at some different systems and techniques.

The Kratky Method

This system is extremely basic—so much so that it is outdated and only used in classroom experiments or by beginners who want to dip their feet into hydroponic gardening. It is a fun way to experiment with the kids. One of the main principles of hydroponics is that all you need is a jar.

A mason jar is an excellent choice for properly positioning your plant or plants in the nutrient solution. Ensure that the leaf portion faces away from the solution while the roots are submerged in it.

This can easily be achieved by using a grid, mesh pot, or the shape of the container. It's a straightforward process that requires only keeping the stem and leaves away from the nutrient solution. Basically plop a stem in some water and nutrients and watch it grow.

Aeroponics

Believe it or not, Aeroponic has been around for quite some time, 1957 to be exact. This system is made up of a series of pipes to send pressurized nutrient solutions to the plants.

When the nutrients pass through the nozzle, droplets are sprayed onto the roots, allowing the roots to breathe freely and receive water and nutrients.

Aeroponics is one of the systems I use for herbs and lettuce, and I am thrilled with its productivity and efficiency.

In aeroponics, crops are watered for brief periods and at frequent intervals. The specific timing of each cycle is determined by the crop and environment and the amount of pressure applied within the system.

There are two pressure systems used in aeroponics: HPA (high-pressure system) and LPA (low-pressure system). For instance, with an HPA, irrigation cycles can be as short as 5 seconds every 5 minutes. This should give you an idea of the difference between ebb and flow or drip irrigation hydroponics.

Aeroponic gardens come in various shapes and sizes and offer significantly greater yields than other hydroponic methods. They are suitable for a wide range of plants. The exceptions are those with extensive and intricate root systems, such as fruit trees, as they are challenging to spray evenly, particularly the central ones. Moreover, the nutrient solution is reused in this technique.

One of the main challenges faced by aeroponics is maintaining stable climate conditions inside the aeroponic chamber, including humidity, temperature, and ventilation.

While this task is relatively easier in large, established locations like a greenhouse, it becomes more difficult in smaller chambers. This is because air is more prone to rapid temperature changes than water and has a lower ability to retain humidity.

Deep Water Culture

These systems are the oldest and historical method of cultivating hydroponic plants. The grow tank serves as a base, containing a nutrient solution and an air pump to supply oxygen to the roots. The roots are immersed in the tank, and incorporating a single air pump allows increased plant growth and promotes aeration of the roots.

This setup is not expensive and has fewer components, reducing the risk of replacements needed. It also allows you to replenish the nutrient solution easily.

One drawback is that the system would require modifications since utilizing a single basic air pump does not effectively aerate the roots. This gardening style is unsuitable for vertical gardens or hydroponic towers and can only be thoroughly cleaned when not in operation. It is also not suitable for plants that cannot stand having their roots wet all the time, like peppers and blackberries.

The Wick System

This ingenious system may not be the top hydroponic choice, but what sets it apart is its ability to tackle many issues of deep-water culture systems with a simple and cost-effective solution. A wick. By dipping the wicks into the reservoir, ensuring they reach the bottom, and placing the other ends in the grow tank, this system requires only a few components: a reservoir, one or more wicks made of absorbent materials like felt or ropes, and a growing medium such as coconut coir or expanded clay.

With a little solution added to the grow tank, the wicks will naturally draw it up from the reservoir as the roots absorb it, much like a plant absorbs nutrients and water.

Nutrient Film Technique

The Nutrient Film Technique (NFT) utilizes a slim layer of nutrients that coats the base of a deep reservoir, nourishing and hydrating the lower roots while allowing the upper roots to breathe.

This method effectively caters to both the upper and lower regions of the roots, resulting in a comprehensive and powerful solution. The most important thing to keep in mind when setting up this type of system is that the grow tank needs to be slightly inclined.

This method conserves water and nutrients while allowing for easy root examination. The roots can be easily removed from the tank and reinserted without causing root damage. Due to the shape of their roots, NFT is not a good choice for larger plants or root vegetables, like carrots, potatoes, or radishes. The tuberous portion of the root is significant, but the smaller roots at the bottom may not provide enough support for the plant to thrive on a thin nutrient film.

Drip System

The drip system offers a remarkable solution to the major issue of aeration. It supplies continuous nourishment and hydration using tubes, pipes, and a growth medium. This approach is closely reminiscent of drip irrigation in traditional gardening.

Pipes and hoses transport the nutrient solution from a reservoir to each plant. The nutrient is then dripped or sprinkled on the growing medium, which releases it slowly. This process allows the homogeneous distribution of the nutrient solution.

The drip system is a great choice for all sorts of plants, including fruit trees. You have full control over how much nutrients you give to each plant, perfect aeration, and low amounts of nutrient solution, which can save you some money. This system is also adaptable to different crop types and plant sizes.

It sounds great, but with its many hoses and pipes, leakage is common but can be a fast fix. If the water pump breaks, you may not notice right away, and your plants will be left without nutrients. Be sure to continue to check on the mechanics of this system. This is the first of two systems I use in my home.

I have a hydroponic tower system which is a vertical gardening setup that maximizes the use of limited space by allowing plants to grow vertically. It is a favorite choice for urbanites or those with restricted outdoor areas yet still desire the joys of gardening.

Ebb and Flow System

One of the primary challenges has been finding ways to transport nutrients and water to plants while ensuring adequate oxygen and aeration. Let's not forget that these roots will need a little spa treatment. The solution that emerged was the ebb and flow system, which involves regularly watering the roots in short bursts. This way, the plants can have periods of oxygenation without being constantly submerged in water or becoming completely dry.

To implement this method, you will mix the necessary ingredients in a reservoir and then use a timer to control when the pump delivers the solution to the grow tank and when it drains it.

The key to determining the irrigation schedule for an ebb and flow system is by understanding the cycle of irrigation and dry phases. Typically, there is a 10–15-minute irrigation phase every two hours of daylight, with a minimum of 5 minutes.

However, this may vary depending on the number of light hours your plants receive, ranging from 9 to 16 cycles a day.

It is important to consider the plants' nutrition and water needs, which change based on light availability and metabolism. In most cases, your system will rest at night.

According to experts, this is a complicated system to set up. Pipes get clogged and break from constant use, and to be frank, it's noisy.

Using this type of system requires a thorough understanding of your plants and their nutritional needs. This also includes their water requirements and humidity preferences. If you are considering experimenting with hydroponic cultivation, it is not advised to begin with this type of setup.

Chapter 7

Choosing the Right Chickens for Your Urban Environment

Choose Your Chicken!

Raising backyard chickens can be rewarding. There is nothing like gathering and cooking fresh eggs in the morning. Given that many urban area ordinances prohibit the raising of poultry within city limits, I won't dwell on this topic for long. Nevertheless, it is beneficial to address it, given that numerous suburban areas permit this practice.

Now, I know what you're thinking: "Chickens in the city? Isn't that against the law?" Well, my friend, that's where the fun begins. You see, while many urban areas give you the evil eye if you so much as cluck at your neighbor, the suburbs are a whole different ball game.

The burbs have the space, the grass, and the sometimes, understanding neighbors. Imagine waking up at the crack of dawn, or let's be honest, a little later because chickens are early risers, and someone has to draw the line. As you step out into your backyard, there they are! Your fluffy butts scratching and pecking their way through the dirt and grass. I can guarantee you will have the freshest eggs you have ever tasted. It's like having your own little piece of farm life!

You may have seen commercials showing carefree families flinging open the gate to a chicken coop, patting one on the head and tossing the chicken feed onto the ground without a care in the world.

But let me tell you that caring for chickens involves effort. It's work, my friend. After opening that door, the chickens may refuse to come out. On the other hand, a few may run out trying to tackle you since you bring their yummy treats. You also won't be sashaying up to the coop wearing your best shoes. You will be watching your step while wearing your mud slingers.

Chicken care begins with water. You must supply the chickens with an ample amount of water, particularly in hot temperatures. Make sure to provide them with a spacious water container that can be easily washed and refilled daily. Honestly, you will need to do this every day to keep them hydrated.

Choose a nutrient-fortified feed. However, do not limit them to just feed!

Chickens are natural foragers, and a variety of treats and scraps will add diversity to their meals. Provide a mix of chopped vegetables, fruits, and kitchen scraps. Grubs and mealworms are an especially tasty treat. Always introduce new foods gradually to avoid upsetting their digestive systems.

Some breeds, like the Buff Orpington, are known for their quiet demeanor. Road Island Red chickens are docile and quiet but not much into snuggling.

The Ameraucana lay beautiful blue eggs, are moderately quiet but scare easily. Leave the rooster behind in an urban environment. They are not needed for egg production.

Choosing the right chickens for your environment is a crucial step in your backyard poultry adventure. You should consider a few key factors to ensure your feathered friends thrive in your limited space and provide you with the benefits you seek.

Temperament is a significant consideration, especially in an urban setting. You want gentle, docile chickens that are somewhat quiet and tolerant of close proximity to humans and other animals. You do not need a rooster for your chicken to produce eggs. They are noisy, and your neighbor will not appreciate a 5 am wake-up call from a rooster. I do not recommend them in a suburban setting. Some breeds known for their friendly personalities include:

Ameraucana

These fluffy are friendly and known for laying beautiful blue-green eggs. They are generally calm and docile, making them well-suited for urban backyards.

Silkies

The Silkie, also known as the Chinese silk chicken, is a unique breed of chicken. It is distinguished by its unusual pom-pom like, fluffy plumage. This soft and delicate feathering is often compared to feeling like silk or satin. The Silkie possesses other distinctive qualities, including black skin and bones, turquoise earlobes, and an extra toe on each foot, setting it apart from most other chickens.
They are known for their calm demeanor and are great mothers. They enjoy cuddles and pampering.

Barred Plymouth Rock

A classic breed, Barred Plymouth Rocks are known for their black and white striped feathers and dependable egg production. They are typically gentle and easy to handle.

Buff Orpington

These docile birds are known for their mellow disposition and beautiful buff-colored feathers. They are excellent brooders, meaning they are good at raising chicks.

Rhode Island Red

Rhode Island Reds are a hardy breed with a calm and friendly nature. They are known for their excellent egg production and ability to tolerate cooler climates.

Wyandotte

Wyandotte's come in various color varieties and are known for their friendly personalities. They are good layers and are adaptable to different climates.

Egg production is another important factor to consider. If you're hoping for a steady supply of fresh eggs, you'll want to choose breeds known for their laying prowess. Some breeds that are known for their high egg production include:

Leghorn

Leghorns are prolific egg layers known for their white eggs. They are active and energetic birds that need a bit more space than some other breeds.

Australorp

Australorps are known for their black feathers and their exceptional egg-laying abilities. They lay large, brown eggs and are relatively calm birds.

Golden Comet

Golden Comets are a hybrid breed that combines high egg production with a friendly temperament. They lay large, brown eggs and are known for their good health.

Space requirements are crucial for urban chicken keepers. Different breeds have different space needs. A good rule of thumb is 15 square feet per chicken. Some breeds are more compact and can comfortably live in smaller coops and runs, while others need more space to roam.

When choosing a breed, consider how much space you can dedicate to your flock. Choose a coop and run adequate for your backyard. Other factors to consider include climate, disease resistance, and availability. For instance, Silkies prefer warmer climates and should be kept dry, while Buff Orpington is a great breed for cold-weather regions.

In addition, choose a breed known for good health with a resistance to common chicken diseases.

Research what breeds are available in your area. Finally, choose a chicken breed that can thrive in your area.

Remember, your chickens are living creatures. You are responsible for their well-being. You must invest time in researching them and understanding the needs of each breed you choose so that you can give them the best possible home.

A Look at the Coop

The coop is the heart of your backyard chicken operation. It is your feathered friend's haven, home, and sanctuary, where they will spend a good chunk of their time. So, it is vital to construct or purchase a pre-made coop that is both comfortable and secure.

But keep in mind chickens are dirty animals! My husband and I were very surprised to find our little balls of puff were pooping machines! A little bit of advice: don't think it's cute to stand chicks on your shoulder or head; they have an incontinence timeframe of about 3 minutes. They will defecate in their water and food and require a lot of care to keep them healthy.

Before you start hammering and sawing, remember that every city has its own set of regulations concerning livestock, including chickens.

Check your local ordinances to confirm that you build your coop according to those regulations. Things like coop size, distance from property lines, and noise restrictions can vary greatly between counties and states. It is best to be properly informed.

Now, let's get down to the nitty-gritty of coop construction. You need to consider if the coop has enough space and can comfortably accommodate your flock. Will they be safe from predators? Is there enough ventilation? A good rule of thumb is to allow 4 square feet of floor space per chicken.

Choose a spot for your coop that is accessible for you and your chickens. Ideally, it should have good drainage, receive at least 4-6 hours of sunlight daily, and be protected from harsh winds and extreme temperatures. If you are in a colder climate, consider placing the coop against a wall or fence to reduce heat loss.

A piece of advice: when setting up your coop, dig deep. Extend wire mesh underground to keep feral cats from using your chickens as a snack. Provide cozy nesting boxes for your hens to lay their eggs. These boxes should be dark and secluded to encourage egg-laying.

Layer the boxes with straw or wood shavings. I suggest sprinkling diatomaceous earth mixed with sand on the coop floor and the run. It will damage the exoskeletons of fleas, ticks, mites, and lice, causing them to dry out and die. Chickens love to take dust baths to keep their feathers clean and free of parasites, so this mixture, plus a shallow container of the mix, will keep your chickies chirping.

Your chickens also need an outdoor area to stretch their wings and free range. Chickens naturally roost on perches, so it's important to provide them with a comfortable perch inside the coop. Use 2x4s or 2x6s, ensuring they are smooth and splinter- free.

Like any home, your coop will need regular maintenance and cleaning to keep it in tip-top shape. Check the coop regularly for any signs of damage or wear and tear.

Clean the coop at least once a week, removing droppings, bedding, and spilled food. Then, put it into your compost bin. Since it is rich in nitrogen, potassium, phosphorus, and other nutrients like calcium, your compost will get a huge boost.

Always wash and disinfect water and food containers frequently. Healthy chickens require a balanced diet. Start with a high-quality commercial feed formulated for laying hens. The feed should provide the essential nutrients the chickens will need for high egg production and overall health.

This will be their primary food source.

I can attest that building a coop for your backyard chickens is a rewarding experience. It allows you to provide a safe and comfortable home for your feathered babies while enjoying the benefits of fresh eggs.

The best part is getting to enjoy watching your feathery friends. It is important to remember that a chicken fortress is more important than a cute coop. Be practical and keep their comfort in mind before you begin this complete project.

When Chickens Aren't an Option

While chickens are usually the first choice for backyard livestock, they are not the only option. If your current circumstances don't allow for a flock of feathered friends, there are other options to explore, such as quail or rabbits. These animals offer a different set of benefits and challenges that are important to consider.

Quail, for instance, are smaller than most bantam- sized chickens and less noisy, making them an excellent choice for urban settings and small spaces. Each quail needs only 1 square foot of space. Up to six can be kept in one rabbit hutch. They are basically the studio apartment dwellers of the bird world.

They are also prolific egg layers, providing you with a steady supply of delicious, nutrient-rich eggs. Speaking of eggs, four quail eggs equal one chicken egg. Quails begin to lay eggs when they are only seven weeks old, as opposed to chickens, which can take up to seven months. However, their smaller size also makes them more vulnerable to predators, so secure housing and netting are essential for their safety.

Quail are not the cuddliest creatures. They are not the type of birds you bring to your shoulder for a friendly chat. They are not big on the whole cuddling thing, either. Think of them as a food supply. They provide eggs and are tasty on the dinner plate, or rather, a dinner plate for one.

Rabbits, on the other hand, are a fantastic option for those seeking a furry hug and companionship. They are social and affectionate creatures that can be easily bonded with and even trained to use a litter box, making them ideal for those who want a more interactive experience with their livestock.

But with all that interaction, you may forget why you are raising them. Since they also provide sustenance, putting them in the stewpot after creating a bond may be difficult.

Rabbit housing can be similar to chicken housing, with spacious hutches that provide protection from the elements and predators.

Follow a healthy diet for rabbits. This will include fresh vegetables, hay, and pellet feed. This type of diet will guarantee they receive the proper nutrients needed while enjoying healthy treats. Your rabbit will also require plenty of fresh, clean water. And don't forget that sanitary cages will help grow healthy rabbits. Whether you choose quail, rabbits, or both, it is important to remember that these animals have specific needs and requirements.

I cannot stress enough to do your research on any animal, pet or livestock, that you choose to raise. Before introducing any animal to your backyard, it is imperative to thoroughly research their required housing, dietary needs, and overall care.

By creating a secure and comfortable habitat for the animals, you will not only reap the benefits of fresh eggs and meat but also experience the satisfaction of nurturing and raising your own livestock.

Chapter 8
Preserving Your Harvest

The practice of homesteading extends beyond the confines of the outdoors, reaching into every aspect of your daily routine. The kitchen is a bustling hub of activity, taking your homesteading experience to another level.

Jars of all shapes and sizes lined my counters, waiting to be filled with our bounty. I carefully washed and prepared the fruits and vegetables at their peak of freshness.

This summer, we harvested over 280 pounds of pears from our two dwarf trees. For the next two years, we are guaranteed to be up to our ears in canned pears, pear sauce, pear preserves, and pear wine.

Stepping into my homestead kitchen, you would immediately notice the heart and soul of my home. The scent of freshly baked bread and the vibrant colors of produce from my garden show in every corner. Braided garlic hangs from a hook on the wall, jars of dried herbs and spices line the shelves, and fresh herbs grow on my windowsill, ready to be added to homemade meals.

This is where the magic happens! It's where the fruits of my labor are transformed into nourishing meals and preserved for the colder months.

Preserving food empowers individuals to be self- sufficient by enabling them to manage their food supply. This reduces the need for store-bought, mass-produced, preservative-laden canned goods and promotes eco-friendly habits by minimizing food waste.

Let's go a bit further on a journey into the world of canning and pickling. We will take a look at the fundamentals, review basic techniques, and embrace the joy of preserving our harvest for the future.

The Fundamentals of Canning and Picking: A Not-So-Dying Art

The canning process is a delicate dance requiring attention to detail. Jars and lids are sterilized, carefully filled with produce, and sealed tightly. The sound of popping lids as the jars cool is music to my ears, letting me know it was a job well done.

Canning is a time-honored tradition that allows us to savor fruits and vegetables far beyond harvest season. It is a wonderful way to preserve our garden's bounty, ensuring a year-round supply of fresh, homegrown produce. Utilizing food from local farmers' markets that you do not have the space to grow can help add to your pantry. Just because you didn't grow it does not mean you can't preserve it.

The canning process involves sealing food in airtight jars, then processing the jars covered in boiling for a water bath or covering a quarter of the jar with water for pressure canning.

The heat brings the jar contents to a temperature that destroys harmful bacteria and seals the jars. This food can be safely stored for years. Canning is a fascinating process that combines science and artistry. Canning allows us to turn fresh produce into a pantry staple to be used later. The core principle lies in creating an environment that inhibits microbial growth, preserving the food's quality and extending its shelf life.

Water Bath Canning: The Basics

Large pots with fitted lids and racks to hold the jars are essential for water bath canning. The process is a careful balance of time and temperature, ensuring the jars are fully submerged in boiling water for the perfect amount of time.

This method is ideal for high-acid foods, such as fruits and pickled vegetables, transforming them into shelf-stable treats.

Each jar is filled with precision, and the produce is packed tightly. The jars are then lowered into the waiting pot. After the allotted time, they are lifted out of the pot and cooled.

Pressure Canning: There is Nothing to Fear

Pressure canning is a type of food preservation that requires a different set of tools. A pressure canner (not a pressure cooker), with its sturdy walls and tight-sealing lid, is necessary for this process. It also uses a lot less water than a water bath canner. Meats, low-acid vegetables, and other delicate produce are prepared, added to jars, and placed in the canner.

Steam will hiss, and the canner will rock, but do not let this deter you. It is perfectly normal part of the process and ensures the contents are safely preserved for future meals.

The process typically involves these key steps:

Preparation:
Begin by selecting high-quality fruits and vegetables that are ripe and free of blemishes. Wash them thoroughly and prepare them according to the recipe. This may involve peeling, blanching, cutting, or pitting, depending on the type of food being canned.

Jar Preparation:
Sterilize the canning jars by running them through the dishwasher or boiling them in a large pot of water for 10 minutes. Wash the lids and rings in hot, soapy water to eliminate any potential contamination.

Packing the Jars:
Carefully pack the prepared food into the sterilized jars. Leave the appropriate amount of headspace as stated in the recipe. Headspace refers to the empty space at the top of the jar. A good way to measure this is by looking at the rings on the jar.

A quarter-inch headspace hits about midway up the jar neck, a half-inch hits just above the bottom ring, and a one-inch headspace hits just below the bottom ring. Fill as suggested in the recipe to ensure proper sealing and pressure regulation during processing.

Processing:
Once the jars are filled, place the lids and rings on them and process them in a boiling water bath or pressure cooker. The processing time varies depending on the type of food being canned and the elevation at which you are canning.

Cooling and Storage:
After processing, carefully remove the jars from the boiling water bath or pressure cooker and allow them to cool completely. As they cool, a satisfying "pop" sound will indicate that a vacuum seal has been created. Store the sealed jars in a cool, dark, and dry place where they can remain safely for years. If the jar does not seal, you can reprocess it with a new lid, freeze it, or place it in the refrigerator for immediate use.

Always select recipes from reputable sources. My favorite is the *Ball Blue Book Guide to Preserving*. I also recommend the *USDA Complete Guide to Home Canning*.

Always follow the recipes carefully, ensure that the processing times and headspace are appropriate for the specific food being canned, and follow the recommended processing time. You don't want to open that can of carrots six months later to find it never sealed and spoiled. There is nothing worse than opening a jar of peaches and finding a weird science experience growing.

Water bath canning is suitable for high-acid foods such as fruits, tomatoes, and pickles.

However, it should never be used to can meat or meat-based products.

Pressure canning is essential for low-acid foods, such as green beans, broths, meats, and poultry, as it generates higher temperatures to destroy potentially harmful bacteria.

Acidity is a critical factor in canning safety. High- acid foods, like fruits and tomatoes, are naturally acidic enough to prevent the growth of harmful bacteria, making them relatively safe to can using the water bath method.

However, low-acid foods, such as beans, vegetables (unless they are pickled), and meat, require a pressure canner to reach the high temperatures necessary to destroy harmful bacteria, preventing botulism, a potentially deadly foodborne illness.

Do not be intimidated by pressure canning. Today's equipment is very safe and easy to use. Canning is a time-honored tradition passed down through generations.

I remember my mother and grandmother's canning jams and how we were able to savor the flavors of summer strawberries long after the garden had wilted away. It is a rewarding process that turns fresh, vibrant produce into jars of soups, jams, and canned vegetables ready to be enjoyed throughout the remainder of the year. Embrace the art of canning, and I promise you that you will not regret it.

Beyond the world of canning, a spectrum of preservation methods awaits, each offering its unique advantages for capturing the flavor of your harvest at its peak.

Pickling: A Symphony of Flavors

Pickling is the art of preserving food in a brine (salt water) or vinegar solution, and it has been practiced for centuries. The brine or vinegar creates a unique and tangy flavor in the vegetable, making a simple carrot a culinary delight. Pickling not only preserves food but also adds a burst of flavor and a satisfying crunch.

Yes, it's true. Pickling remarkably transforms ordinary vegetables into crunchy, tangy delights, and the process is simple. Not to mention it also feeds your digestive system with healthy probiotics and promotes good gut health.

Pickling relies on the acidic nature of vinegar or a salt brine to prevent bacterial growth, creating an environment where food can be safely preserved. The pickling process involves immersing food in a vinegar, salt, or sugar solution and allowing the flavors to infuse and ferment.

Preparing vegetables for pickling involves a similar process to canning. After selecting crisp, fresh produce, washing it, and checking that it is free of blemishes, pack it tightly into sterilized jars and fill it with a brine solution. The brine is the secret to successful pickling.

The next step is where the magic happens. The jars are submerged in boiling water to be processed.

Be sure the jars are completely covered in water.

The heat will then penetrate the jars, sealing in the crispness of the vegetables and allowing the brine to transform the contents. Below are common pickling methods.

Quick Pickling

This method uses a shorter pickling time, often just a few hours or overnight. This will result in a softer texture and a milder flavor.

Fermented Pickling

A traditional method that uses bacteria to ferment the food, creating a tangy and complex flavor. Fermented pickles are often characterized by a softer texture and a distinct sour taste. They should not be canned. High temperatures will kill the good bacteria.

Preparing for Pickling

Before you embark on your pickling journey, here are some essential tips:

Cleanliness is Key

Sterilize all jars, lids, and rings properly to prevent contamination and ensure safe preservation.

Choosing the Right Produce
Select firm, fresh produce without bruises or signs of spoilage. Avoid overripe vegetables.

Balancing Flavors
Adjust the recipe to your taste with spices to create your desired flavor profile. Do not change the vinegar or sugar measurement. The method of measurement for the recipe ensures its safe preservation.

Pickling Vegetable

There is nothing like eating a dilly bean in winter, making vegetables a popular pickling choice. The acidic brine transforms their texture and flavor. Here's a guide to vegetables that are great for pickling:

Cucumbers - Cucumbers are a classic pickling vegetable. The crisp texture and mild flavor are only enhanced by the pickling process.

Carrots - Pickled carrots can be enjoyed as a snack or in salads and sandwiches. Carrots add sweetness and a vibrant orange shade when added to pickles.

Onions - Onions add a pungent flavor to pickles. Pickled onions can be used on sandwiches, salads, and burgers.

Other Vegetables - Other vegetables, such as cauliflower, green beans, and peppers, can also be pickled, adding a unique twist to your pickling repertoire.

Pickling Fruits

Believe it or not, fruit can also be pickled. It may sound like a crazy idea, but pickling fruit creates a sweet and tangy treat that can be enjoyed on its own or used for desserts and cocktails. Below is a guide to fruits that can withstand the pickling process:

Peaches - Peaches offer a juicy and flavorful pickling experience. If you have never had a pickled peach, you are missing out. They can be enjoyed as a dessert or used for salads and desserts.

Cherries - Cherries add a vibrant red hue and are tart sweetness after pickling. Pickled cherries can be enjoyed as a snack or used to give a cocktail or dessert an extra pop of flavor.

Other Fruits - Other fruits, such as pears, apples, and berries, can also be pickled. They add a unique flavor experience to any dish.

Chapter 9

Dehydrating, Freezing, and Freeze Drying: The Basics

Dehydrating

Dehydrating is another preservation art I am attempting to master. Thin slices of fruit and vegetables are laid out on trays and slowly dried in the oven or dehydrator to create delicious snacks and ingredients for future meals. This technique removes all moisture from the food inhibiting bacterial growth, and prolonging shelf life.

The art of dehydrating food is a cornerstone of this homesteader's kitchen and ensures a constant supply of nutritious snacks and ingredients.

Thinly sliced fruits and vegetables are laid out with precision on trays, each piece carefully selected to ensure only the freshest produce is used.

The gentle buzz of the dehydrator fills the room as it works tirelessly in the background, slowly drawing out the moisture. The process is a delicate balance, requiring the right temperature and timing to ensure the perfect result. As the hours pass, the produce transforms, its vibrant colors intensifying and its texture becoming crisp.

Dehydrating intensifies flavors and transforms fruits and vegetables into portable, nutritious snacks. I experiment with dehydrating apples, creating delicious, crunchy chips, and drying tomatoes, resulting in a concentrated burst of flavor for future pasta dishes.

Once complete, the trays are carefully unloaded, and the now-dried fruits and vegetables are stored in airtight containers. The variety of goods that can be dehydrated is a testament to the skill and creativity of our ancestors. Crispy apple chips, chewy banana slices, and tangy strips of dehydrated citrus peel provide a rainbow of flavors.

Vegetables are not left out of this method, with carrots, beets, celery, and even broccoli transformed into tasty, portable snacks that are ready to be enjoyed anytime.

Dehydration is a centuries-old method of preservation. It harnesses the heat from the sun or by using specialized equipment to remove moisture from foods, significantly extending their shelf life.

The result is a concentrated, flavorful, and lightweight product that can be rehydrated or enjoyed as is.

The Science of Dehydration

Dehydration works by reducing the water content of food, making it an inhospitable environment for bacteria and enzymes to grow. The dehydration process preserves food and also concentrates flavors and nutrients, creating a unique and delicious experience.

The following are common food-dehydrating methods:

Sun Drying

This traditional method utilizes the sun's natural heat to remove moisture from food. It requires warm, sunny conditions and a well-ventilated area to ensure proper drying.

Food Dehydrators

Electric food dehydrators offer consistent and controllable drying conditions, allowing you to dehydrate a wide range of fruits, vegetables, herbs, and even meats, think jerky.

Preparing for Dehydration

Before embarking on your dehydrating adventures here are some essential tips:

Start with Freshness - Choose produce that is at its peak of freshness, free from blemishes, or has signs of soft spots or bruises.

Prepare for Drying - Wash and slice your fruits and vegetables into thin, even pieces for optimal drying. Some fruits, like apples and pears, or vegetables, like turnips and potatoes, may require blanching before drying to prevent browning.

Drying Time Varies - Drying time depends on the type of food, thickness of slices, and humidity levels. Check your food frequently for doneness, ensuring it is dry and leathery.

Dehydrating Fruits

Fruits are ideal candidates for dehydration, as their sweetness and flavor intensify during the process. Below is a guide to dehydrating various fruits:

Berries - Berries like strawberries, raspberries, blueberries, and blackberries can be dehydrated whole or sliced. Dehydrated berries can be enjoyed as a healthy snack or used for baking.

Stone Fruits - Peaches, nectarines, plums, and cherries can be dehydrated by slicing or halving them. Remove the pits and slice thinly for faster drying.

Tropical Fruits - Mangoes, pineapples, and bananas can be dehydrated after peeling and slicing. Dehydrated tropical fruits offer a unique and exotic flavor.

Dehydrating Vegetables - Vegetables can also be dehydrated, adding versatility and flavor to your pantry.

Dehydrating Vegetables
Dehydrated vegetables can be used for soups, stews, and snacks. Here is a guide to dehydrating different vegetable types:

Leafy Greens - Greens like spinach, kale, and chard can be dehydrated after blanching and chopping. Dehydrated greens can be used for soups, sauces, and stews. Or throw a combination of dried greens into the food processor until it is a powder.

Add the powdered greens to any meal you want to give a nutrient packed boost.

Root Vegetables - Carrots, potatoes, and beets can dehydrate after peeling and slicing. Dehydrated root vegetables can be used for soups, stews, and snacks.

Other Vegetables - Broccoli, cauliflower, green beans, and mushrooms can be dehydrated after blanching and chopping.

Dehydrating Herbs

Dehydrating herbs is a simple and effective way to preserve their flavor and aroma. Here is how to dehydrate herbs:

Hanging Method

Wash and dry the herbs. Tie the herbs together by the stems. Hang in a warm, well-ventilated area until dry. Store in an airtight container.

Dehydrator

Wash and dry herbs thoroughly. Strip leaves from stems and lay them in a single layer on dehydrating trays.

Dehydrated herbs can be stored in airtight containers for up to a year.

Freezing: Nature's Pause Button

Freezing is the ultimate time-bender, preserving fruits, vegetables, and even herbs right at their peak of freshness. It's a simple and versatile method that often requires minimal preparation. Imagine biting into a juicy strawberry plucked fresh from your garden.

Now imagine eating that strawberry and it tasting just as sweet and juicy in the dead of winter. Freezing allows you to relive that experience, capturing the vibrant flavors and textures of summer's bounty.

The Art of Freezing

Freezing relies on the principle of lowering the temperature to below the freezing point of water, effectively stopping the growth of bacteria and enzymes that cause food to spoil. The key to successful freezing is to freeze rapidly, which will minimize ice crystal formation, which can damage cell structure and affect texture.

Preparing for Freezing

One of the simplest and cost-effective ways of preserving food is through freezing. Individual portions, like berries, can be flash frozen by arranging them in a single layer with no contact between them then freezing them separately before combining them for extended storage in the freezer.

Flash freezing enables the option to defrost and warm single servings instead of thawing out entire food containers.

There are a few essential steps to ensure optimal preservation:

Selection is Key

Choose produce at its prime! Overripe fruits and vegetables will not freeze well and can have an undesirable taste.

Blanching: A Vital Step

Blanching is a crucial step for certain vegetables, like broccoli, green beans, and peas. This quick dip in boiling water for 30 to 60 seconds is followed by an ice bath that immediately stops the cooking process. Blanching helps preserve color, texture, and flavor while also destroying enzymes that can cause yucky freezer flavor.

Packaging Matters

Utilize freezer safe bags or containers, ensuring they are tightly sealed to prevent freezer burn, a condition that causes dehydration and flavor loss. Label your packages with the date and contents for easy organization and identification.

Freezing Fruits - Fruits are particularly well suited for freezing. Their sweetness and juiciness are often enhanced after a stint in the freezer. Here is a short guide to freezing some of the most common fruits.

Berries - Berries like strawberries, raspberries, blueberries, and blackberries are very freezer-friendly. Wash, dry, and flash freeze them whole on a baking sheet before final storage, or lightly crush or puree them before freezing.

Stone Fruits - Peaches, nectarines, plums, and cherries can be frozen whole, halved, or sliced. Wash well, remove the pits, and freeze in a single layer on a baking sheet before transferring them to freezer bags.

Citrus Fruits - While not as commonly frozen, citrus fruits like lemons, limes, and oranges can be frozen as juice, zest, or wedges. To freeze juice, place it in ice cube trays for easy portioning.

Freezing vegetables follows the same protocol.

Freezing Vegetables- Vegetables are a fantastic addition to your freezer repertoire, adding convenience and versatility to your meals.

Leafy Greens- Greens like spinach, kale, and chard can be frozen after blanching and chopping. Pack them tightly in freezer bags, squeezing out excess air.

Root Vegetables - Carrots, potatoes, and beets can be flash-frozen after peeling and chopping. Blanching is optional but recommended to maintain texture and color.

Other Vegetables - Broccoli, cauliflower, green beans, peas, and corn can be frozen after blanching and chopping. Pack them tightly in freezer bags or containers.

Freezing Herbs - Fresh herbs like parsley, cilantro, basil, and thyme can be frozen for use throughout the year. Chopped herbs can be frozen in ice cube trays with water or oil for easy portioning ready to be added to stir-fries, soups, and sauces.

Freeze Drying: The Future of Preserving

Another fairly new but remarkable preservation method is freeze drying. Freeze drying is a unique method of preserving food that not only extends its shelf life but also maintains its original flavor and aroma. The process involves freezing the food and placing it in a vacuum, where the ice is directly converted into gas without turning back into a liquid.

Freeze drying ensures that the original smell and taste are not lost in the preservation process. The result is lightweight, easy-to-store food with an incredibly long shelf life that looks and tastes fresh when rehydrated.

Freeze drying is a popular choice for preserving delicate herbs and spices, transforming fruits into perfect crisp snacks, and adding to cereals and yogurt.

Unlike dehydrators, a freeze dryer comes with a hefty price tag. Beginning at $1500, they can range up to $5000 depending on size and capacity.

However, part of homesteading is using what you have and reaching out to others in your community.

A wonderful couple from the church owns this coveted device. They generously offered to freeze dry a large pear harvest I had. I offered them a part of the harvest, and they freeze-dried my prepared pears. It was the beginning of a mutually beneficial partnership that continues today.

If you do not know anyone who owns a freeze dryer, don't worry. There are other options than breaking the bank. Look it up online. Many people offer to freeze-dry your produce for a rental fee.

Others ask for a portion of your bounty. You do not have to own every piece of equipment to homestead.

Again, think outside the box. Freeze-drying opens new possibilities for preserving your harvest. The power to extend my garden's shelf-life and reduce waste brings me a sense of fulfillment. It's a satisfying journey into just a small part of homesteading.

Freezing, dehydrating, freezing, and pickling are techniques that have been passed down through generations. It allows us to connect with history while savoring the bounty of our gardens long after the growing season has passed.

Chapter 10

Cooking from Scratch

The Joy of Your Harvest: A Year- Round Feast

Whether you pickle, freeze, can, dehydrate, or freeze dry, these techniques are more than just preservation techniques; they celebrate our harvest, help us become more self-sufficient, and promote a healthier lifestyle. Imagine opening a jar of vibrant tomato sauce in the middle of winter, the aroma of basil and garlic filling your kitchen.

Or savoring the sweetness of peaches preserved in their prime. Snacking on a chewy dried apple or snacking on those dilly green beans. Maybe rehydrating those potatoes to their former glory with a little bit of water.

Even the eggs we get from local chickens are preserved in our home by freeze-drying, water glassing, or dehydrating. We are confident that we will have a constant supply of protein throughout the year.

"Putting up" clean, preservative-free food allows us to enjoy the fruits of our labor throughout the year, bringing a touch of homegrown goodness to our table.

Lets take a look at a few ways to make the most of your harvest.

Building a Well-Stocked Pantry

Canning helps us create a pantry filled with flavorful and nutritious ingredients, ensuring we have healthy options on hand for meals and snacks.

Share the Bounty

Gifting jars of homegrown preserves is a beautiful way to share the joy of the harvest with friends and loved ones. Christmas Pears are a big hit with our friends and, with some fabric and ribbon, make a wonderful housewarming gift.

Create Delicious Dishes

Use your canned produce to create a wide variety of dishes, from hearty soups and stews to desserts. Once you have mastered your pressure canning, research recipes for jar canning recipes and have dinner ready in a matter of minutes.

Let's savor the flavors of our garden, knowing that we are preserving not just food, but a legacy of flavor for generations to come.

During my homesteading journey I found satisfaction in making meals from scratch. In the kitchen, homemade bread and preserves come to life. It is a place where one can embrace their creativity, experiment with new recipes, and feed their families wholesome goodness. Bake that bread from scratch! Prep and cook your meals at home using whole, unprocessed ingredients, and forget junk-filled fast food! Take satisfaction in what you accomplished. Become a culinary warrior princess (or prince).

Throw away the processed food and embrace a healthier way of feeding your family. It is a well-known fact that preparing meals at home not only helps you save money but also promotes better health compared to fast food options.

When following a recipe that claims to take 30 minutes, it's important to allow yourself 60 minutes when just starting out and be okay with this extra time. Learning how to cook and bake takes patience and practice.

However, once it becomes a regular part of your routine, you will notice a significant improvement in your speed and efficiency. By choosing to cook your meals from scratch, you control the ingredients you use; you control what goes into your food, resulting in a healthier lifestyle for you and your loved ones.

There are so many wonderful recipes available online. Even simple recipes can be delicious. You can also check out recipe books from the library or borrow a friend's favorite cookbook.

Start with the basics.

Dishes like pasta soup or grilled meats with less than seven ingredients. Roast vegetables; it only takes a pan of oil and your prepared vegetables in a 425 °F oven.

Create a meal plan.

This will allow you to have your ingredients on hand and not have to change your plans. There is also peace of mind in knowing exactly what you will cook that day.

Keep your pantry stocked.

Keep your pantry stocked. We just went over preserving food. Use them! Keep flour, sugar, salt, rice, and butter on hand.

Use seasonal items.

Use seasonal ingredients. Strawberries in June are a whole lot sweeter than in December. Using fruits and vegetables that are in season will result in fresher, less processed foods.

Don't waste.

Use everything in your refrigerator. Part of homesteading is turning those wilting vegetables into a tasty broth or that leftover chicken into chicken salad for tomorrow's lunch.

Double your recipe.
That is pretty clear. Make twice as much. It will take no extra time. Then put half away in the freezer or can it if it is a big batch of chili or soup and have your own version of frozen dinners.

Become a prepper.
Prepping will put you way ahead of the week. Take an hour or two to do all your prep work: chop, dice, and shred. Then, after a long day at work, you will have all your ingredients.

Oh yes, the joys of preserving and creating magical meals from scratch. Let me tell you, there is one kitchen gadget that has been my saving grace.

When it comes to preparing rice, it doesn't get any easier than a rice cooker, my friend. Invest in one of those bad boys, and you will save yourself from the frustration of overcooked or undercooked rice. No sticky mess, but perfectly fluffy rice every time. It's like having your very own rice-cooking genie! If you purchase one that also steams vegetables, you are golden.

Speaking of kitchen gadgets, I have also embraced the art of slow cooking. My trusty crockpot has become my partner in crime for those days when I want a hearty, home-cooked meal but don't have the time or energy to babysit a pot of simmering stew.

Not that preparing a pot of stew on the stovetop isn't satisfying; I really enjoy the process. But on those busy days when you can toss everything into a crockpot and let it work its magic while you go about your day, it's a no-brainer.

The handy-dandy food processor is like having an extra pair of hands in the kitchen, ready to chop, slice, and dice at the push of a button. Whether whipping up a batch of fresh pesto with basil from my garden or making a zesty salsa, I can always count on my food processor as my trusted sidekick. Chopping onions and mincing garlic can be a tedious task. That is where a food processor comes to the rescue! It transforms prep time from a chore to a breeze.

With the right attachments, you can shred mountains of cheese, grate cabbage or zucchini, slice potatoes, and carrots, and even finely chop herbs for that roast in seconds.

This homesteading life may not always be easy, but it sure is rewarding. Here's to embracing the simple joys, getting our hands dirty, and creating delicious memories, one meal at a time.

Chapter 11

All Things Dairy

The art of creating cheese is a delicate balance of science, measuring, and time. You must be patient! Follow each recipe specifically, and do not take any shortcuts. If the recipe instructs you to stir in a figure-eight motion, for 2 minutes, set that time, grit your teeth, and stir those curds and whey even if it feels like your arm will fall off, or it could end up a lumpy, tasteless mess. Just do it. First and foremost, you will get the cleanest, healthiest, and best-tasting cheese you ever had. You will control the level of sharpness and dryness your cheddar wheel will become. Let's start with basic information about cheese making.

The cheese-making process starts with warming the milk to the perfect temperature for the microbes to work their magic. Each cheese type has its own high temperature to reach. Too much heat can lead to tough and rubbery cheese.

Cultures are added, and the milk curds are formed. This process generally takes around an hour to develop the deep flavors. Once the curds have set, they're cut with a curd knife (a round-tip metal knife) and then strained. From this point on, the curds will differ depending on the type of cheese you are making. Hard cheese, like cheddar, is then wrapped in a cheesecloth and placed into a cheese press, while soft cheese can be whipped until creamy and spreadable.

For cream cheese, I gently stir in a culture of bacteria, watching as the milk thickens and transforms into a creamy, spreadable delight. But for ricotta, I take a different approach. I carefully heat the milk, adding a touch of acid to encourage curdling until it is delicate and fine, soft, fluffy ricotta.

Mozzarella, however, needs a more hands-on approach. After the curds are formed and drained and sit for a couple of hours, they need to be stretched and folded, being worked like dough until they become shiny and elastic. The result is a cheese perfect for shredding and melting over freshly made pizza dough.

Environmentally speaking, aging cheese requires specific temperatures and humidity after being wrapped and pressed. Most cheeses are aged between 50°F and 55°F with 85% humidity. However, some cheeses are aged cooler or warmer and at varying humidity levels.

Having What It Takes

Do you have what it takes to become a hobby cheesemaker? We talked about patience and following exact directions. Now, let's talk about the ingredients: milk, culture, and salt.

That's it? Yes and no. You can choose between raw milk and store-bought milk. An array of cultures is available to make different types of cheese, but since we are sticking with the basics, we will focus on the most common cultures.

Raw milk is milk that comes from cows, goats, or other animals and has not been pasteurized or homogenized. Prior to the 1900s, all milk was consumed raw.

After an outbreak of bovine tuberculosis, the process of milk pasteurization began. Pasteurizing milk involves heating it to 161°F for 15 seconds. Homogenizing is a process of applying extreme pressure to disperse the fatty acids more evenly, improving appearance and taste.

Raw milk contains the lactase-producing bacteria called Lactobacillus, which is destroyed during pasteurization. It is said that raw milk improves lactose digestion and contains just about all the natural cultures needed to make cheese. The microbes in raw milk can make everything from parmesan to brie and are in that same cup of raw fresh milk.

The type of cheese made is determined by how the curds are treated during the cheesemaking process, as powdered starter cultures are added to inoculate pasteurized milk.

However, government studies state that raw milk, with its neutral pH, high nutritional and water content, and possible contact with unsanitary udders, feces, or other animal body parts, can be a feeding ground for bacteria. Purists argue that pasteurized milk has higher levels of protein, fatty acids, nutrients, and calcium.

You decide which type of milk you use. I only caution against using ultra-pasteurized milk. As the temperature of the milk rises, for ultra-pasteurized milk it is 280°F, the more likely that the microbes will become completely destroyed, making it difficult to transform the milk into a creamy cheese.

Moving on to cultures, there are several to be aware of:

Mesophilic culture - Approximately 75% of all cheeses can be made by using just two cultures. The mesophilic culture is a type of acidifying cheese culture that ripens at temperatures around 86°F. It is commonly used to create Cheddar, Colby Jack, Brie, Queso Fresco, Havarti, and Blue Cheese, to name a few.

Thermophilic culture -The second type of cheese culture used is the thermophilic culture. This is another type of acidifying cheese culture that ripens at temperatures over 100°F. It is typically used to make cultured Mozzarella, Parmesan, and Asiago, among other cheeses.

Propionic Shermanii -this culture, also known as Swiss culture, is used forAlpine-style cheeses like Swiss are made with propionic Shermanii. When added, it produces the characteristic "eyes" and unique flavor found in Swiss cheese. Propionic Shermanii does not produce acid on its own and must be used with either a thermophilic or mesophilic starter culture.

Rennet - Rennet is a natural enzyme extracted from the stomach of a young calf. It is commonly used in cheesemaking to help curds form and separate them from the liquid whey. While traditional rennet is extracted from animal sources, vegetable rennet options are now available.

This type of culture is made by culturing genetically modified bacteria specifically bred to produce the enzyme.

I did some research for a more natural option and found that there really is plant-based rennet. By cutting the stem from a fig tree and removing the white sap can be used in place of animal rennet, but it may result in weaker curds, giving you a softer cheese.

Citric acid - Citric acid is another acid source used in cheesemaking. It can be used as a shortcut for making uncultured mozzarella or cheeses like paneer. Using citric acid will require patience, as it's known to take all day for the curds to acidify.

Vinegar -The acid from vinegar or lemon juice can be used in a pinch to make softer cheeses like cream cheese or ricotta. However, it may affect the cheese's flavors.

Cheese Salt

When making cheese, it is important to use a simple, additive-free salt known as cheese salt. Iodized salt can react with the cheese, and most types of grocery store salt contain anti-caking agents and additives. The whole point of making our own cheese is to keep it free of additives.

If you need to substitute cheese salt, pure kosher or pickling/canning salt can be found in most supermarkets. These salts are pure and do not contain any preservatives that may negatively affect the cheese. However, be sure to check the labels.

As I further explored the world of cheesemaking, I studied more advanced techniques. I experimented with different bacteria and enzymes and played with time and temperatures to create unique flavors and textures.

The possibilities are endless. But before you become the next cheesemaker extraordinaire, you need to learn and practice the basics until you have mastered them. Otherwise, you will waste a lot of ingredients, which is a complete contradiction of the homesteader mindset.

Easy Cheesy

Let's make some cheese! Gemma Stafford of *Gemma's Bolder Baking* inspired this cream cheese recipe; it was the first I ever made.

Cream Cheese

6 cups (32 oz /1000 ml) whole milk 3 tablespoons lemon juice
½ teaspoon cheese salt or canning salt
Using a heavy saucepan, heat the milk on medium heat, stirring constantly until it starts to a gentle simmer. Do not let the milk come to a boil. I have been there, done that, and got the T-shirt. Your cheese will end up clumpy and rainy.

Reduce the heat to medium. Add the lemon juice one tablespoon at a time, with about a minute between each tablespoon. Continue stirring constantly.

Continue simmering gently. The mixture will curdle. Stir constantly until the mixture has separated completely. This will take a few minutes. The curdles will rise to the top, while the whey will remain on the bottom of the pot.

Whey is a nutrient-dense byproduct and one of the two main proteins in milk. It is translucent and slightly yellow.

Remove from the heat.

Line a colander with cheesecloth and place it over a large bowl to catch the whey. Pour the curds into the cheese close. Let it strain and cool for about 15 minutes.
Once it has cooled, pick up the cheesecloth, twist the ends together, and squeeze the excess whey out of the curds.

Transfer curds to a food processor and process for 2 to 4 minutes until smooth and creamy. If the cheese is too stiff, add a splash of the whey or cream and blend again.

Add salt to taste. The cheese can be stored in the refrigerator for up to 7 days.

Another beginner cheese to try is ricotta. The process is similar to making cream cheese with different acid, vinegar. Once the curds are strained, they go into a container and are ready to be eaten or added to a recipe.

The next "level" up in cheese making is cultured mozzarella. Below is a basic mozzarella cheese recipe using a gallon of milk. Remember that you can use raw or pasteurized milk.

In addition, many cheese kits are sold that include everything you need to make one or two batches of cheese. I highly recommend starting out with a kit.

Mozzarella Cheese

1 gallon whole milk
1 ¼ cups water
1 ½ teaspoons Citric Acid
1/4 teaspoon liquid rennet or 1/2 rennet tablet and one teaspoon kosher salt

Measure 1 cup of water and stir in the citric acid until dissolved. Then, measure 1/4 cup of water into a separate bowl. Stir in the rennet until dissolved.

Pour the milk into the pot and add the citric acid solution. Stir while heating the pot over medium-high heat until milk temperature reaches 90F.

Remove the pot from heat and gently stir in the rennet. Stir while counting to 30. Cover the pot and let it quietly sit for 5 minutes.

After five minutes, the milk should have set. It should look and feel like soft, silken tofu. If it is still more liquid than curds, place the lid onto the pot and let it sit for another five minutes. Once the milk has set, cut the curds into uniform squares. Make several parallel cuts slicing vertically through the curds and then several parallel cuts slicing horizontally, creating a grid-like pattern.

Be sure your knife reaches all the way to the bottom of the pan.

Place the pot back on the stove and warm the curds to 105°F over medium heat. Slowly stir the curds, but try not to break them up too much. Eventually, the curds will clump together and separate more from the whey.

Remove the curds from the pot and place them into a microwave-safe bowl with a slotted spoon.

Microwave the curds for one minute. Drain off the whey into another bowl. Put on your heavy rubber gloves and fold the curds over onto themselves a few times. At this point, the curds will be very soft and resemble cottage cheese.

Microwave the curds for another 30 seconds, checking the internal temperature until it reaches 135°F. Begin pulling and stretching the curds again. They must reach this temperature to stretch properly.

Sprinkle salt over the cheese and squish it into the cheese mixture using your fingers to incorporate. With both hands, stretch and fold the curds until they start to tighten. The mozzarella will become firm and take on a glossy sheen. When this happens, it's time to shape the mozzarella. Now comes the cheese maker's choice.

You can make one large ball, two smaller balls, or several bite-sized bocconcini. But do not overwork the cheese. If you are not using it right away, refrigerate by placing the mozzarella in a small container and covering it with a teaspoon of salt and a cup of cool whey. Cover and refrigerate. The mozzarella can be kept refrigerated for up to a week.

Once you begin to feel more comfortable with the process, try your hand at other types of cheeses.

When I made my first round of cheddar, I was so excited I shared it with all my friends, even if they didn't want to try it. I couldn't get over the fact that not only did it look like "real" cheese, but it tasted like it, too!

Making your own cheese gives you a great sense of pride and accomplishment, and you will not want to go back to store-bought cheese again.

Available online are cheese kits that include cultures, presses, and rennet, depending on the type of cheese you wish to make. It takes the guesswork out of your ingredient purchase.

Yogurt

The process of making yogurt is equally exciting. I simply love making my own yogurt. Some milk, a culture, and a little bit of time results in a creamy, delicious yogurt. Add some fresh fruit or raw honey for a delectable snack. It is perfect for enjoying on its own or using as a base for even more creative dairy-based recipes such as dips or in place of sour cream.

Simple Yogurt

1 gallon of milk
1/4 cup plain store-bought yogurt (you read that correctly)
Digital or candy thermometer
Plastic or wooden spoon (do NOT use metal)

Start by slowly heating the milk to 180°F. This temperature encourages the growth of the bacteria that will thicken the milk and give it that characteristic tang. An enamel cast iron is perfect for maintaining the heat.

Remove from heat and let sit until the milk temperature drops to 115°F.

Gently pour some of the heated milk into the yogurt to temper it, then stir it into the yogurt.

Maintain a temperature of 115 °F until the milk solidifies. Since this can take up to 12 hours, you can wrap the pot in towels to keep it warm. I put my covered pot into the dehydrator and set it to 115°F for 10 hours.

Line a colander with a good quality cheesecloth and place securely over a bowl.

Carefully pour the yogurt into the cheesecloth to drain the whey. Depending on how thick you like your yogurt, this could take up to three hours. If the yogurt gets too thick, stir in some whey until it reaches your desired consistency.

Scrape the sides of the cheesecloth and stir the yogurt. Place in mason jars or other lidded containers. Rinse out your cheesecloth to use again. Experiment with different fruits and sweeteners each time you dish out this yummy treat.

Yogurt can be refrigerated for up to 2 weeks.

Butter

Yes, you can make your own butter, and it's pretty simple. You can even include the kids in the process. The key to successful butter-making is to separate the fat molecules from the liquid. This can be done by agitating the cream. A high-powered blender or a Mason jar can be used. There is another way: using a stand mixer.

Butter

1 pint heavy cream
1/2 teaspoon kosher salt
Begin by combining the cream and salt in the stand mixer, starting at a low speed and gradually increasing it until it reaches level 8. After about 3 minutes, the cream will begin to thicken and resemble whipped cream. Cover the top lightly with a dish towel to help avoid a mess when the butter begins splashing.

Continue whipping the cream for about two minutes. At this time, you should begin to hear wet plopping or a sploosh. This is a good indicator that the cream has separated into solid fat and liquid buttermilk.

Lift the towel, then carefully pour off as much buttermilk as possible. I stored it in a jar in the refrigerator.

Collect the butter into a large ball and rinse it in a bowl with ice water, squeezing out as much of the buttermilk as possible.

Empty the bowl and replace it with clean ice water. Repeat this process six to seven times until the water runs clear after squeezing. You want the butter to run clear because any remaining buttermilk will cause it to taste rancid.

Next, add the salt and work it into the butter.

Finally, pat the butter dry with a paper towel before placing it in a butter crock or roll it into a log and wrap it in parchment, wax paper, or plastic wrap. Your homemade butter will be rich and creamy and resemble the yellow color of Irish butter.

The blender method can be difficult to clean but follows the same steps as a stand mixer.

Add half the ingredients as the stand mixer recipe for the Mason jar method. This process can be exhausting. Try recruiting some mini scientists (the kids) for the task and adding a science lesson. Then, let them go to town, taking turns shaking the jar.

When it clumps up, remove the butter and follow the steps for rinsing the butter indicated in the recipe. It's also a sneaky way of tiring them out.

The Whey We Were

Remember all that whey from the cheese and yogurt I told you to pour into other bowls and containers and save? It is because Whey is a powerhouse of nutrition. You can replace this nourishing liquid with any recipe that requires water, providing an extra boost of enzymes, protein, and minerals. By soaking grains or legumes in whey and water it can also aid in digestion.

Whey from cheese made with vinegar or lemon juice will produce acid whey. It will have a tangy flavor, while whey made with rennet or other cultures will be sweet.

You can incorporate whey into a variety of dishes, such as smoothies, pancakes, grits, and bread dough, or even use it as a cooking liquid for rice. Additionally, you can safely give it to your pet for added nutrients.

Whey has many uses, including diluting it in water and feeding it to plants or to yourself.

It can also help amend your soil pH and is even used by some to soften their hair. If you don't plan on using it within a few days, you can freeze the whey. Don't discard it; keep your whey!

Chapter 12

Sourdough Bread 101

When I began cooking and baking from scratch, I came across a LOT of sourdough recipes. There was so much hype about it contributing to good gut health and how it helps with digestion. And best of all, no yeast was required.

The wild fermentation produced its own "wild yeast." All these recipes I came across mentioned using a sourdough starter. So, I looked online to purchase one of these starters.

There certainly was a lot to choose from! Then I came across a sidebar titled "Make your own sourdough starter." Hmm, I thought, no ordering online from a strange source, and I know what is going into my starter. It was then that I decided to take the plunge into the world of sourdough.

I was determined to avoid any potential pitfalls. I wanted my sourdough journey to be a smooth ride without gloppy flour messes that resembled paper mâché glue being tossed into the trash.

I gathered all my ingredients, measured out my flour and warm water, mixed them together, and carefully followed the directions so that my starter had the perfect environment to thrive. Every day, I checked my starter, discarded half, fed it more flour and water, and waited until the next feeding. My life revolved around a 12-hour mark. I'd found myself glancing at the clock, thinking, "Almost time to feed my little lactobacilli family!" I didn't want to risk those bacteria dying and my time and efforts being wasted.

The beige concoction bubbled and grew in my mason jar. I got so excited! I finally baked my first loaf. I thought I followed the directions perfectly. I imagined that crusty, tangy sourdough bread coming out of my oven perfectly round and fluffy.

Well, it was round. It was dense and not very fluffy at all. In fact, it had hardly risen. It was a complete failure. I gave up and decided it was too much work keeping the starter alive and far too much flour wasted. I dumped it in the trash.

What I didn't know back then was that there were different techniques.to making sourdough bread as opposed to making regular yeast bread.

I learned that you could make small-batch starters thanks to Melissa Norris from *Pioneering Today*. I also learned that I should not have dumped half the starter every time it was fed.

The "discard" from the starter can be used in so many other baked goods. At this point, it is not strong enough to raise bread and hasn't developed that classic sour taste. By adding it to your pancakes, muffins, brownies, or even your zucchini bread, you are adding a boost of good bacteria to your belly without affecting the taste of your baked goods.

One of my frustrations was the thought of constantly feeding it. My family likes sourdough bread, but not every day. It didn't seem viable for me to continually feed the starter.

I discovered that you can actually put your starter to sleep by putting it in the refrigerator. It slows down the fermenting, requiring a once-a-week feeding schedule. There is a process to using that starter. It will need to be removed from the refrigerator, and flour and water must be added for about 48 hours before being used to bake.

Sourdough making is a craft, and like all crafts, it takes a lot of practice to master.

Making the Starter

Flour

What is the perfect flour for a nutritious sourdough loaf? It varies with different tastes and opinions.

Each flour presents its own benefits. Bread flour is high in protein and promises excellent elasticity, structure, and volume.

Unbleached All-Purpose flour is versatile, softer, and has a more tender crumble.

Whole grains, like whole wheat, rye, and spelt each have distinct differences.

Rye flour is earthy and has a slightly sour flavor.

Spelt flour is rich with a nutty taste and aroma.

Whole wheat is a nutritional powerhouse, containing the most protein, healthy fats, vitamins, and minerals of all flours.

What you choose depends on your personal preference of taste and texture. It also includes what is most important to you to have in your bread.

Organic flour free of glyphosate and bromate is recommended. Once you have the hang of sourdough baking, you can craft your own blend and create your unique sourdough starter that can quite possibly be passed down through your family.

Supplies

For me, glass and wood utensils are the way to go. I personally do not use plastic containers since I don't want any more nanoplastics or microplastics added to my body than I need to.

Plastic releases small amounts of bisphenol A (BPA) and dioxin into the food. Some studies have linked these pollutants to lung disorders and heart disease, among other illnesses.

I have also read opposing opinions on using any kind of metal, including utensils, to stir it. Reactive metals like aluminum and copper can give your bread an off taste and harm the yeast fermentation. The only metal you should use is stainless steel.

Glass is recommended to store the starter.

What you will need:
1 quart jar -   Glass jars, or pottery, or stainless steel.
Rubber band or string

Cheesecloth
A wooden spoon or spatula for mixing.
Kitchen scale or Measuring cups
Flour
Water

How to Create and Feed Your Sourdough Starter

Ingredients
30 grams or
¼ cup flour
30 grams or 2 Tablespoons of warm water

Directions for Making and Feeding Sourdough Starter

Mix together flour and water. Use the same type of flour for each feeding. Place the cheesecloth on top of the jar and secure it with a rubber band or string.

The ideal water temperature is between 65° F and 70° F. Every 12 hours, discard half your starter and feed it again using ¼ cup (30 grams) of flour and 2 Tablespoons (30 grams) of water.

Feeding your starter about 12 hours apart, but don't stress over it. It will not ruin the mixture if you are a little early or late.

The next day, remove half the starter (yes, remove it!). You must remove the discard so the bacteria can grow. Feed it again using ¼ cup (30 grams) of flour and 2 Tablespoons (30 grams) of water.

Continue this procedure through the first week, scraping down the sides and bottom of the jar.

The best temperature for your starter is 70° to 85° F. If your home is cooler, place the jar near a heat source, not on it, so it stays warm and does not cook.

In the early stages, around the third day, your starter will likely begin to smell yeasty, tangy, sour, or even like alcohol.

By day 6, you can start feeding once a day, but continue to remove the discard. If the bubbles aren't rising and seem to be dying down, put it on a twice-a-day feeding schedule.

Once the starter hits week 4, it should have doubled in size. It is now ready to be used in bread recipes.

How to tell if your Starter is Active

You should begin to see bubbles start to develop on the top and sides of the jar after the first couple of feedings. The top will dome after the feeding, and a few hours later, it should double in size. This is an indication that the lactobacilli bacteria is multiplying. By the next feed time, a liquid will be on top of the mixture. It's basically saying, "Hey, I ate all that yummy sugar, and I'm ready for some more flour!"

How to tell if your Starter is in Crisis

If any dark brown or pink shows in the starter, they have been contaminated and need to be tossed. If a putrid odor is present, check for a layer of liquid (hooch) on top, as it can indicate the yeast's state of being alive or dying and may require attention. Revisiting the starters' original feeding schedule is in order.

Understanding the Process

Let's begin with the basics. Before we can begin baking sourdough bread, we need to understand what makes it tick. What is a sourdough starter? What is wild yeast? What is sourdough discard?

Let's jump into the fascinating world of sourdough and uncover the secrets behind this ancient craft.

Understanding the fundamentals is key to mastering the art of sourdough bread making.

So, what exactly is a sourdough starter? How does it differ from your average commercial yeast?

Well, let's imagine a magical mixture of flour and water, teeming with wild yeast and friendly bacteria, creating a bubbly concoction that is full of life. This starter is the heart and soul of sourdough, contributing to its unique tangy flavor and airy texture.

When you combine equal parts of fresh flour and water, the yeast and bacteria, both in the air and on the flour, will begin a fermentation process, transforming the mixture into an active leavening agent.

Now, you might be wondering, what is so special about wild yeast? Unlike its domesticated cousin, commercial yeast, wild yeast naturally occurs and can be found floating all around us. It is this wild yeast, along with the bacteria in the starter, that gives sourdough its distinctive characteristics. As the yeast feasts on the sugars in the flour, it produces carbon dioxide, creating those beautiful air pockets that make the bread rise.

But what is this about sourdough discard? Well, my friend, that is one of the little quirks of sourdough baking. You see, to keep your starter happy and healthy, you will need to feed it regularly with fresh flour and water.

Over time, you will end up with more starter than you need, and that's where discard comes in. It might sound wasteful, but trust me, it is not! At least it's not when you know not to throw it away.

Sourdough discard is simply the portion of the starter that you remove before feeding. And it is far from being useless. In fact, it can be used to create delicious treats, from pancakes to crackers and even donuts!

Making a sourdough starter can take 5 to 7 days. Sometimes for up to 2 weeks. This is a commitment, so be patient. It is not a project to start on a whim, thinking you will be able to make sourdough bread the next day.

Gluten-Free Option

Gluten-free sourdough bread is possible, my fellow gluten-intolerant friends. You can bake a delicious and satisfying gluten-free sourdough loaf following the same process.

Creating a tasty gluten-free sourdough bread can be a bit more challenging than creating a traditional version. However, with practice and experimentation, creating a satisfying and mouthwatering sourdough loaf is absolutely achievable.

Be patient (there's that word again), as your gluten- free sourdough starter may require more time than a traditional starter to become active and develop its bubble action.

The chlorine in city water may kill or inhibit the growth of wild yeast and good bacteria. Therefore, it is recommended that you use filtered water in your starter.

The chlorine in city water can kill or inhibit the wild yeast and good bacteria growth.

When it comes to traditional sourdough, the taste and texture are all about personal preference. The same applies to a gluten-free version.

You have the option of using a gluten-free flour blend or exploring other options like hearty brown rice or nutty buckwheat. Keep in mind that buckwheat takes the longest time of these flours to ferment.

Perhaps you could try using sweet rice flour. For an extra boost of healthy fats and fiber, consider adding a flaxseed meal to your bread dough once you begin baking your bread.

Just as it is all about your preference for the taste and texture of a traditional sourdough, the same is true for your gluten-free version. You could use a gluten-free flour blend, but there are other options, such as hearty brown rice or buckwheat.

Buckwheat has a wonderful nutty flavor but takes the longest to ferment. Perhaps you would prefer sweet rice flour?

Once you begin baking your bread, you can even throw some flaxseed meal into the dough recipe for extra fats and fiber.

Baking the Bread

About 12 hours before you plan to mix the dough,
add to a clean jar:
1/2 cup starter
1 cup water
1 cup flour

Mix and allow this to sit covered at room
temperature for 8-12 hours to double in size.

Ingredients
3 cups room-temperature water 2
½ teaspoons salt
1 cup sourdough starter
6 cups bread flour

Mix water and salt together in a large bowl. Add sourdough
starter and whisk to mix and aerate.

Add 2 cups bread flour and stir until smooth.

Slowly stir in the remaining 4 cups of bread flour
until the dough is completely mixed.

Cover bowl and set aside until dough bubbles and increases
in volume.

After about 12 hours, turn the dough onto a well-floured surface using floured hands. Turn the dough several times to cover it with flour. Pull one end of the dough upward, then fold it to the center. Turn your bowl a quarter around, pull that end upward, and fold it over to the center. Do this twice more.

Place the dough in an oiled bowl and let it rest for 2 to 3 hours until it has doubled in size.

Preheat oven to 450° F. Place an 8-quart Dutch with the lid in the oven for 30 minutes.

Gently roll the dough out of the oiled bowl onto parchment paper, gently placing it into the Dutch oven, and cover it.

Bake in the preheated oven for 30 minutes. Remove the lid and continue baking for another 15 minutes until the crust is golden brown.

Carefully lift the loaf out of the Dutch oven using the corners of the parchment paper.

Slide off the parchment and onto a cooling rack.

Cool completely before slicing.

Bread should have a hollow sound when tapping on the bottom of the loaf.

Simple Gluten-Free Sourdough Bread

This recipe is easy, has just four ingredients, but takes 2 days to make.

3/4 cup 1:1 Sourdough starter (do not feed)
1 ¼ cup water
3 ¼ cups 1-1 Gluten Free Flour Mix with Xanthan Gum
1 ½ teaspoon salt
Oil

Day 1

Add the starter, 1:1 gluten-free flour, water, and salt to the bowl of a stand mixer. Using the dough hook, mix all ingredients until they are combined. The dough should come together without any loose flour left.

Gently form the dough into a ball and place it in a lightly oiled and floured bowl. Cover and leave in a draft-free place for 6-10 hours. You want the dough to begin to rise but not double in size.

After the first rise, place the bowl in the refrigerator to finish proofing for 12 hours.

Day 2

Heat oven to 500° F and place Dutch oven inside preheated oven for 30 minutes.

Remove the dough from the refrigerator and roll it out onto a lightly floured piece of parchment paper.

Gently reshape the dough with flour, covering the entire ball with flour.

Remove the Dutch oven and place the dough and parchment paper into the Dutch oven.

With a sharp knife, slash an X about an inch deep in the center of the loaf.

Cover with a lid, place in the oven on the center rack, and lower the temperature to 450° F for 40 minutes.

Remove the lid, lower the temperature to 425° F, and bake for an additional 40 minutes.

Remove the Dutch oven and pull the bread out using the parchment paper corners.

Slip off the parchment paper and onto a cooling rack.

Cool Completely before slicing.

As your confidence grows, you may even create your own signature sourdough. Making sourdough is a challenge, but with patience and practice, you can create mouthwatering breads that cater to all your dietary needs.

So, embrace the process! Soon, you will be sharing your sourdough masterpieces with family and friends.

Chapter 13

Natural Cleaners: Scrubbing Solutions

Moving beyond the kitchen, let's look at natural cleaning solutions. If you want a healthy and toxic- free environment, try homemade cleaners and soaps crafted by you. It can be so simple: A capful of vinegar will clean the grim off your floors, and a little olive oil on a cloth will shine up your stainless steel.

We can't forget the power of baking soda. It cleans drains and scrubs away dirt without scratching.

The right combination makes it an eco-friendly, dynamic cleaner that is resistant to germs and toxins.

While store-bought cleaners are generally the go-to solution for many people, do not underestimate the power of homemade cleaners. They can be just as effective.

However, it is important to note that, depending on the level of dirt, some surfaces may require a bit more scrubbing or a second application for the best results.

Also, keep in mind that not all homemade cleaners are suitable for every cleaning job or surface, even if labeled as "all-purpose." For instance, you do not want to use an acidic cleaner on granite or ammonia on aluminum.

Not too long ago, I discovered a whole new world of natural cleaning solutions. I found myself in a world of vinegar, borax, baking soda, and essential oils.

I began concocting homemade cleaners that would give Mr. Clean a run for his money (not really).

My secret weapon? Vinegar, that trusty sidekick that tackles grime like a superhero. All it takes is a gallon of water and a little vinegar.

DIY Cleaners

Here are a few simple recipes:

All Purpose Cleaner

Water

White Vinegar

Orange Peel or Lemon Peel

Spring Rosemary or Mint

Combine all the ingredients and stir well. Add to a spray bottle and let it sit for a week. You now have a powerful cleaner for showers, sinks, and countertops.

Air Freshener

Spray Bottle

Water Essential

Oil Baking

Soda

Fill a spray bottle with water. Combine one tablespoon of baking soda and six drops of your favorite essential oil into a bowl. Once combined, add the mixture to the water. You now have a natural, non-toxic air freshener.

Furniture Polish
1/2 cup White Vinegar
1/2 cup Olive Oil

Mix the ingredients in a bowl. Dip a microfiber cloth into the solution and gently rub it onto your wood surfaces.

Aside from being budget-friendly and better for the environment, homemade cleaning products give you the power to regulate the amount of chemicals and components used in your home. There are so many cleaner recipes out there, from laundry detergent to soap scum removers.

Take one step at a time. Create one cleaner and try it in your home. Part of homesteading is making changes to better your life. But you do not have to jump in with both feet. Sometimes, it's okay to dip your toes in the water and see what suits your lifestyle.

If you do not want the challenge of making cleaners, try purchasing natural cleaners like castile soap. I use this on everything: floors, laundry, and toilets. It has a delightful peppermint scent and is made with natural oils. There are some wonderful environmentally friendly cleaners on the market.

If you want to help lower your carbon footprint, try switching from paper products to linen. I am not suggesting giving up toilet paper for the leaves in the backyard.

Rather, try replacing the paper napkins with fabric ones. Make them yourself out of inexpensive cotton to save money.

Use dish towels and wash rags to clean up the spills instead of relying on paper towels. Then, toss everything into the washing machine. Small changes will eventually lead to big results.

Homemade Soaps: Understanding the Process

Each winter, I attempt to learn another skill. Two years ago, I decided that. I wanted to create beautiful and luxurious bars of soap that I could wow my friends and family with. I imagined bars of soap that were perfectly colored and scented and felt soft and creamy on my skin.

But my journey was slow. Some creations came out wonderful, but others did not retain their scent. They were too small or too bumpy. I shared a bit of my stock with friends, and my family used the rest. But I could not seem to graduate from melt-and-pour soups to hot press or cold press techniques. And that was okay. We are not going to be great at every skill. For me, understanding the process of soap making if SHTF is what matters to me the most. But that doesn't mean I can't ever try again.

My suggestion is to start with melt-and-pour soap bases. You can choose from a variety of bases, from goat's milk to glycerin. Adding essential oils gives your soap a wonderful scent.

You can also add herbs, oats, and even coffee to your soap. Mica is ideal for coloring your soap without staining your skin, and essential oils can be incorporated for scent. Melt, mix, and pour into molds, and that's all there is to it.

However, there is another layer to soap making. Some may call the melt-and-pour method "cheating" and say it isn't true soap making. And they may be right since there are also in-depth soap-making skills to consider and learn.

When making lye soap, a transformation called saponification takes place. It is a chemical reaction that converts the oils into soap. Both techniques require the use of lye. To make a "true soap you will need fat+liquid+lye. Many are uncertain about using lye since it is dangerous if handled incorrectly.

Always wear eye protection and gloves on your hands. Your work area should be well-ventilated and clean. Keep a bottle of white vinegar nearby to neutralize the lye mixture if it should spill or splatter on anything.

Finally, since lye is acidic before it is mixed in oil or water, you will want to keep all your ingredients ready to combine easily, quickly, and distraction- free. If you follow the correct safety measures, you will not have a problem.

First is **'cold process' soap**. Although heat is initially required at the beginning of the process to melt solid ingredients, after this step, there is no further heating.

Once the melted solid oils and all the other ingredients are mixed together, the soap is left to cure for at least four weeks. Many think this process is easier than the hot process of soap.

Supplies Needed

A crock pot or a stainless-steel pot (this should be designated for soap-making)

Immersion blender

Digital Scale

Eye protection and gloves

Containers for mixing ingredients

Heatproof container for mixing lye

Wooden or metal spoon and Spatula

Soap mold

Ingredients

15 oz coconut oil

17 oz olive oil

4.5 oz of 100% lye (Sodium Hydroxide) 12 oz of water

2 tsp herbs and/or 1 oz of essential oil (optional)

Parchment Paper

Directions

Start by melting your coconut oil in your pan in the microwave or crock pot.

Put on your protective glasses and gloves. Carefully measure the lye and water separately and pour the water into the heat-proof container. Slowly add the lye to the water (NEVER ADD WATER TO THE LYE; YES, IT MATTERS). Stir carefully.

As you stir, the mixture will become cloudy, white, and very hot. Allow the mixture to cool for about 10 minutes. The mixture will become clear as it cools.

After the coconut oil has melted, pour it into a separate bowl, add the olive oil, and allow it to cool.

Pour the water and lye mixture into the oils and stir using a metal or wooden spoon.

At this point, you will want to rinse the container used for the water and lye mixture, then re-rinse with white vinegar to make sure all the Lye has been neutralized.

Use the immersion blender to blend for about 4-5 minutes or until it is opaque and the mixture starts to thicken. You are looking for the mixture to come to "trace." This is when the soap mixture has the consistency of pudding and holds its shape after plopping a spoonful on top.
This is when you will add your herbs and essential oils.

Quickly and carefully spoon into a mold lined with parchment paper. Then, cover the mold with more parchment paper and let it cool in a dry place where it will not be disturbed.

After 48 hours, using gloves, remove the soap from the mold and cut it into bars. At this point, they will be sticky.

The bars need to cure for about four weeks. You can place them on paper bags or drying racks and turn them every few days to allow complete drying.

Then you have **'hot-pressed' soap**. Many prefer this method since curing is optional, but if it is not cured, it will not last as long or be as hard. Hot- process soap only takes about 2 weeks to cure.

However, it is not as smooth as cold-process soap. The supplies are the same as cold-process soap.

Ingredients

20 oz Coconut Oil

10 oz Olive Oil

4.78 oz Lye

9 oz water

2 tsp herbs and/or 1 oz of essential oil (optional)

Parchment Paper (if not using silicone molds)

Directions

Start by melting the coconut oil in your pan, in the microwave, or a crock pot.

Once the coconut oil has completely melted, add olive oil.

Put on your protective glasses and gloves. Carefully measure the lye and water separately and pour the water into the heat-proof container. Slowly add the lye to the water and stir carefully.

Pour the water and lye mixture (after complexly dissolved) into the oils and stir using the silicon or wooden spoon.

With the crockpot on low, use the immersion blender to blend and stir until the mixture is opaque and starts to thicken. Use short pulses. It will thicken quickly.

Once it comes to trace, place the lid on the crockpot and continue to heat on low for 50 minutes. Keep an eye on the crockpot and make sure it doesn't bubble over. If it begins to, give it a quick stir

Quickly and carefully spoon into a mold lined with parchment paper. Smooth out the top and press it into the corners of the mold.

Place it in a cool, dry place where it will not be

disturbed to cool for 24 hours.

Using gloves, remove the soap from the mold and cut it into bars. Allow to dry for another 24 hours to harden.

You can now use the soap or let it cure for another 2 weeks.

All the ingredients needed to create your own soaps can be found online. A quick search will bring up hundreds of options. Starter kits with very easy-to-follow instructions are also available.

As I sit here writing this chapter on soap, I have decided to give it, pull out my supplies, and attempt the hot process method. I know what I said earlier! I don't need to know how to do everything.

But there are so many lovely soap recipes online; some soaps look like a work of art.

Maybe, just maybe, I can give soap-making another try. I hope you do as well.

Chapter 14

Utilizing Sustainable Sources

Solar: Unleashing Sun Power

It's not uncommon for people to desire to harness the power of the sun. Solar energy is often seen as a costly project. Why should we consider utilizing solar energy in urban areas? Have you ever thought that living in an apartment limits your option of switching to a solar grid?

To begin using solar power, you do not need a complete overhaul of your home power grid to implement solar energy into your daily life. Small changes are all that are required.

Let me explain: By utilizing solar cookers and dehydrators, we can take advantage of the sun's energy to prepare our food and preserve our produce.

This allows the free opportunity for eco-friendly cooking techniques, such as cooking, steaming, or boiling any dish that can typically be prepared in a conventional oven. It may take longer, and you will need to periodically reposition the oven to ensure even cooking with a renewable energy source, but reducing your carbon footprint is worthwhile.

Additionally, rooftop solar panels have been gaining popularity for rooftop gardens. Irrigation systems, greenhouses, and other farming equipment need to be powered.

Instead of running cords over the fire escape or down the access stairway to a power source, a portable solar station or solar generator can get the job done.

Portable solar-powered pumps can be used in rain barrels to help the water circulate and prevent stagnation, as well as provide an eco-friendly solution for irrigation.

Ventilation is crucial in greenhouse environments, and running fans during the day can help circulate the air and keep the temperature perfect for plant growth. A solar generator with a solar panel will keep the greenhouse functioning correctly.

Localize heating by using a solar-powered heat mat can provide enough warmth for seedling trays. As for your everyday needs, solar energy can be used to charge phones and other electronic devices. Use a backup battery and hang portable solar panels off the balcony to charge your freezer. Portable systems are ideal for small spaces, especially during a blackout or crisis.

Have I successfully convinced you? Solar

power can be incorporated into your urban homesteading, even without complete control over your selection of power providers. Sometimes, it only takes small steps to make big changes in your lifestyle.

Rain Harvesting

Imagine your city filled with rooftop gardens capturing rainwater, nourishing thriving raised beds, and vertical gardens. This can become a reality for you. You can avoid the broken food system in this country and focus on fixing it by homesteading and supporting small-town farming.

We live in a world where water is an increasingly precious resource. The practice of rainwater harvesting has become popular among eco- enthusiasts and homeowners.

What is rain harvesting? It is the collection and storage of rain. The rainwater is captured instead of being allowed to run off the roof and used at a later time.

With a growing water crisis in many states, people are eager to look for sustainable solutions, and rainwater harvesting is a promising option.

However, with so many varying state regulations on rainwater catchments, many find themselves navigating through a web of legalities.

The residents of Colorado, for instance, are permitted to collect rainwater but with a strict maximum capacity of 110 gallons. This limit presents a challenge for those seeking to become water- resilient.

In other states, such as Oregon, Arkansas,

Utah, Washington, and Kansas, permits are required before residents are allowed to install rainwater catchments, adding a layer of bureaucracy to the process.

Despite these restrictions, the core message remains that rainwater harvesting is not an illegal practice. No federal laws or restrictions prevent the collection of rainwater.

Although varying state legislations can cause some confusion, and social media tends to blur the truth at times, it leaves many wondering if their efforts to conserve water are, in fact, compliant with the law.

There are many states where water harvesting is encouraged. In fact, rebates and grants are offered for rainwater collection and promoting sustainable water practices. Let's take a look at the benefits of harvesting rain.

Just one inch of rain on a 500-square-foot roof produces 300 gallons of runoff. By harnessing rainwater for non-drinking purposes such as flushing the toilet, watering the garden, and using it for laundry, households can substantially reduce their water bills.

Speaking of watering gardens, using rainwater to irrigate the garden will improve plant growth and overall health since rainwater is free from many chemicals found in tap water, like chlorine and fluoride.

Rainwater collection alleviates the strain on the city's water resources and provides a viable and eco-friendly option.

Having a backup water source can be valuable in an emergency or crisis if city water supplies are disrupted or wells run dry.

However, there is a downside. Depending on the system you choose, it can result in a large upfront financial investment. If you plan to use it for drinking water or cooking, a filtration system must be added to the cost. You will need space for the storage tank or barrels. Depending on where you live, it may not be viable in an urban environment. Rainwater harvesting systems, filters, and roof gutters will need regular cleaning to prevent contamination.

Well, folks, if you're still with me and interested in diving into the world of rainwater harvesting, sit back, get a beverage, and let's explore the ins and outs of putting together your very own rain catchment system!

Building Your System

First things first, you will need proper equipment. The core of your project will be a sturdy water storage tank or rain barrels. Of course, the size of your tank will depend on state regulations and your own personal needs. Catchments can hold 50 to well over 250 gallons of water. Your location, space, and intentions will help you determine which type will suit your needs.

Equipment
Barrel or water Tank with spigot
Barrel stand or pavers to elevate
Downspout
Leaf catcher lid
Submergible pump (optional)
Down Spout

Once you have all your supplies, you will need a way to direct the rainwater into your storage system. Causing a neighborhood flood with misdirected water will not earn you the Neighbor of the Year award.

You could easily gather rainwater by placing multiple buckets outside to catch the falling rain. However, the rain must be redirected into a designated catchment area to collect a substantial amount of water. This can be done using the downspout and connecting it to the gutter system on your roof. If the downspout is longer than the height of your rain barrel, it may need to be trimmed to ensure proper water flow.

Catchment

The barrel or tank you have chosen will need to be positioned beneath the downspout to capture the runoff from the gutter. Elevate the tank off the ground so there is easy access to the spout. Once elevated, gravity will help the water flow freely out of the spout.

Be sure the container has a secure mesh lid to prevent debris and insects from entering the tank.

Setting Up the System

If you intend to use rainwater for non-potable purposes, no further action is required unless you would like to install a pump to disperse water to your garden. A solution to avoid this expense would be to extend one of the house's other downspouts directly into the garden instead.

Utilizing the harvested rain for consumption, such as flushing toilets or washing dishes, will involve more equipment. You might want to consider adding a filtration system to remove contaminants and leave you with clean, usable H2O.

Equipment and parts can be found at many big-box hardware stores. If you do not want the hassle of putting one together yourself, there are a variety of kits available. Let your fingers do the walking— over your keyboard and onto the internet. Equipment and kit options await you.

Conclusion

The journey of urban homesteading is not always easy. It takes dedication, creativity, and a willingness to fail. If you do fail, you dust yourself off and try again. As you move forward in your journey, embrace the spirit of urban homesteading, fostering a more sustainable, resilient, and connected way of life for future generations.

Your future of urban homesteading does not have to be a distant dream. It is a growing movement taking root in cities across the globe. From community gardens to rooftop farms, urban homesteaders' creativity and resilience are transforming their urban spaces into thriving mini-farms.

You can find happiness in simplicity and fulfillment. Through homesteading, you can connect to nature. Every time you learn a new skill, you gain power, and with this power, you will discover true freedom.

I can attest that this lifestyle can become addictive. Know when to stop and know when to rest. Do not exhaust yourself or set unrealistic goals or timeframes for projects.

As your journey into urban homesteading progresses, commit to this mindset: **Start where you are and do what you can.**

Acknowledgments

This book would not have been possible without the support and inspiration of my family and friends (you know who you are) and their unwavering encouragement and patience during the writing process.

My family's belief in my vision and willingness to go along with each little change I have made over the years, from switching from paper to fabric napkins to tasting my "new and improved" herbal remedies, has given me the confidence and courage to keep moving forward.

I am also deeply grateful to the countless online and in-person urban homesteaders who shared their stories and experiences and provided daily insights and inspiration. Their passion for sustainable living and innovative approaches to homesteading are truly inspiring not only in limited spaces but also in all spaces.

Finally, I want to acknowledge the many resources, books, and articles that have shaped my understanding of homesteading in general.

The knowledge and experiences shared by the homesteading online community have been instrumental in my journey and all that I have learned.

References

Admant, Ashley (2021, January 8). Beginners Guide to Cheesemaking." Practical Self Reliance." https://practicleselfreliance.com/beginner-cheesemaking

Brehm, Emily (2019, June 1) Transgenerational Effects of Endocrine-Disrupting Chemicals on Male and Female Reproduction 160(6):1421-1435 10. "National Institute for Health." https://pubmed.ncbi.nlminih.gov/30998239

Bulla, Andriano (2022, April 7). 7 Different Types of Hydroponic Systems and How They Work. "Gardening Chores." https://Gardiningchores.com/types-of-hydroponic- systems

Kingry, K. and Devine, L. *Ball Complete Book of Home Preserving* Ontario, Rose Rose Inc., 2020

Norris, Melissa (2021, January 15) How to Make a Sourdough Starter + Tips for Success "Pioneering Today." https://melissaknorris.com/podcast/5-tips-on-how-to-get-started-with-sourdough/

Stafford, Gemma (2025, January11)) Same Day Sourdough Recipe. "Gemm's Bigger Bolder Baking"
https://biggerbolderbaking.com/same-day-sourdough-bread
Vartan, Starre (2024, May 30) A Beginners Guide to Rainwater Harvesting. "Treehugger." https://www.treehugger.com/beginners-guide-to-rainwater-harvesting

Zac, Jeremiah (2024, August 7) Is it Illegal to Collect Rainwater: 2024 Complete State Guide. "World Water

Reserve." https://worldwaterreserve.com/is-it-illegal-to-collect-rainwater

USDA Complete Guide to Home Canning, (2015 revision) "National Agricultural Library." https://www.nal.usda.gov/exhibits/ipd/canning/items/show/101

Author Biography

Hi, my name is Renee McCorry. I am the mom of two adult children, a "well-cared-for" dog, and a new Grandma. I am married to the most patient man in the world, who puts up with my rollercoaster writing and experimental homesteading ideas.

I have been writing since middle school and was a small-town newspaper writer for a few years. Although I have always loved cooking, canning, and gardening, I began seriously homesteading during the COVID-19 pandemic.

Using online sources, studies, and books on homesteading, I added garden boxes and raised beds piece by piece to my suburban backyard. All the while, implementing small changes slowly in the kitchen that led to big lifestyle changes. My family's self-sufficiency grows a little more every day, and with a little effort and a lot of work, I know yours can, too.

I'd love for you to tell me what you think of *Urban Homestead: Starting Where You Are* by reaching out to me at www.leafandlores.com. **I would be honored if you took the time to leave a review!**

I hope you enjoyed this book enough to refer it to a friend. Be on the lookout for other books.

Check out *6 Ways to Live a More Self-Reliant Life* and *The Farm Girls' Journal: 90 Days of Love, Hope, and Faith*